I0430077

Congressional
Research
Service

Contemporary Developments in Presidential Elections

Kevin J. Coleman
Analyst in Elections

R. Sam Garrett
Specialist in American National Government

Thomas H. Neale
Specialist American National Government

October 18, 2012

Congressional Research Service

7-5700

www.crs.gov

R42139

CRS Report for Congress
Prepared for Members and Committees of Congress

Summary

This report considers contemporary developments in presidential elections. It emphasizes three topics chosen for their recurring importance and notable recent developments: (1) nominating procedures; (2) campaign finance; and (3) the electoral college. The report highlights significant developments in these areas, particularly for the 2008 and 2012 elections. It also provides background information about the presidential election process in general. Other CRS products cited throughout this report provide additional information about the topics introduced here.

As the report notes, 2012 was expected to be a noteworthy election cycle for several reasons. Some are extensions of developments that started in 2008 or before, while others are more recent. Key themes discussed in this report include the following:

- In recent years, the two major political parties have made efforts to control the "front-loading" phenomenon, the tendency for states to vie to be first or among the first to hold caucuses or primary elections to select presidential nominees. As the result of inter-party cooperation following the 2008 election, front-loading was significantly reduced for 2012.

- Among Republicans, the winner-take-all method that had been widely used was replaced with a proportional system for contests before April 1, although strict proportional allocation was not mandated. With an open race for the Republican nomination, the pace of primaries and caucuses and the new allocation rule were expected to have an unpredictable effect. In the end, the changes prolonged the contest in comparison to recent previous contests.

- Significant changes in campaign finance law shaped campaign finance in the 2012 election cycle, largely as a result of the 2010 Supreme Court decision in *Citizens United v. Federal Election Commission*. In the aftermath of *Citizens United*, presidential candidates may face additional pressure to raise funds to be able to compete against their opponents and outside groups, particularly new organizations called "super PACs."

- One of the most notable campaign finance developments in recent elections is the decline of the public financing system for presidential candidates. The 2012 cycle marked the first since the public financing program's inception that no major candidate accepted public funds.

- After decades of congressional inactivity, state-level initiatives to reform the electoral college were actively considered in 2012. Among these were proposals to establish the district system of awarding electoral votes in Pennsylvania and Wisconsin and further discussion of the National Popular Vote initiative (NPV). NPV seeks to implement direct popular election of the President and Vice President through an interstate compact, rather than by constitutional amendment.

- Various states have considered or are considering changes to their participation in the electoral college. Moreover, a nongovernmental organization, the National Popular Vote (NPV) campaign, has proposed an interstate compact that would achieve direct election without a constitutional amendment.

This report will be updated periodically throughout the 2012 election cycle.

Contents

Figures

Tables

Contacts

Introduction

Presidential elections are among the most iconic events in American politics. Particularly before the television era, campaigns for the presidency and vice presidency were relatively brief events, involving a small band of supporters and occupying only a few months of the election-year calendar. Today, presidential campaigns last months or years, involve thousands of professional employees and volunteers, and are the preeminent political event of a four-year cycle. Since the mid-19th century, certain elements of the role of political parties, money, and nomination procedures have remained constant, but many have evolved with time.

This report considers contemporary developments in presidential elections. It emphasizes three topics chosen for their recurring importance and notable recent developments: (1) nominating procedures; (2) campaign finance; and (3) the electoral college. The report highlights significant developments in these areas, particularly as they relate to the 2008 and 2012 elections. These topics have obvious political implications that affect the race for the presidency. They are also modern manifestations of the democratic process in the United States. Key issues include how the party nominees are selected, which are financially able to compete in elections and how, and whether electors or voters should ultimately be responsible for electing the nation's chief executive.

All these concerns may be of interest to Congress as Members continue to follow and be involved in presidential campaigns, participate as delegates to the national conventions, and potentially consider their own presidential candidacies, but also as the House and Senate oversee federal elections and consider various reform proposals. The report proceeds by discussing the nomination process, which starts the presidential contest. It then considers campaign finance, the raising and spending of funds that are vital throughout the nomination and general election process. The final section addresses proposed changes affecting the electoral college, the final step in electing the President. A preview of major points appears below.

The presidential primary season is often shaped by events in the previous election cycle. That was especially true for 2012. After years of negotiations, the national Democratic and Republican parties reached agreement on a plan to organize the schedule of primaries and caucuses and reduce front-loading. In recent election cycles, the Iowa and New Hampshire contests had been pushed from February into January, under pressure from other states that sought a place at the beginning of the process. Democratic party rules usually kept these states from jumping ahead of Iowa and New Hampshire, but did not prevent a rush to schedule early events within the rules. Inter-party cooperation averted a similar result for 2012, which featured a significantly less front-loaded calendar.

Another development that shaped the nominating contest was a change to the Republican rules for awarding delegates according to the presidential vote. The winner-take-all method that had been widely used was replaced with a proportional system for contests before April 1, although strict proportional allocation was not mandated. With an open race for the Republican nomination, the pace of primaries and caucuses and the new allocation rule had an important effect by extending the contest in comparison to past nominating seasons.

Significant changes in campaign finance law are expected to shape campaign finance in the 2012 election cycle. Most prominently, this includes developments resulting from the Supreme Court's 2010 decision in *Citizens United v. Federal Election Commission*. In that case, the Court invalidated long-standing prohibitions on corporations and unions using their general treasury funds to make independent expenditures calling for election or defeat of specific candidates. (Direct contributions from corporate and union treasuries remain prohibited.[1]) These changes apply to both presidential elections and other campaigns. In the aftermath of *Citizens United*, presidential candidates face additional pressure to raise funds to be able to compete against their opponents and outside groups, particularly new organizations called "super PACs." In addition to *Citizens United*, the future of the presidential public financing program is in doubt, as candidates increasingly opt instead for private funds.

The electoral college method of presidential elections has long been the subject of discussion. To critics, it is archaic, anti-democratic, and has, on four occasions, elected Presidents who received fewer popular votes than their opponents. To defenders, it is a pillar of federalism, promoting inclusive candidacies and a moderate two-party system. Between 1948 and 1979, Congress considered numerous constitutional amendments to reform the system or replace it with direct election, but no single proposal ever gained the constitutionally required two-thirds majority of both chambers needed to submit an amendment for state ratification. After decades of inactivity, the issue is enjoying a revival, as various states consider reform on the sub-federal level. Moreover, a nongovernmental organization, the National Popular Vote (NPV) campaign, has proposed an interstate compact that would achieve direct election without a constitutional amendment. The compact would bind signatory states to award their electoral votes to the nationwide popular vote winner, notwithstanding results within the state, and would take effect after states controlling more than half (270) of electoral votes agree. By late 2011, eight states and the District of Columbia, possessing a total of 132 electoral votes, had joined the compact.

To summarize, the three major areas discussed in this report—the nominating process, campaign finance, and the electoral college—have been central elements of presidential elections for over a century and a half. Each of those areas has experienced transition in recent decades, but each is also facing changes particularly relevant for the 2012 election cycle.

- Both Democrats and Republicans amended their nomination processes to reduce front-loading and bring more order to the nomination process. For the first time, the two parties agreed on a window during which primaries are permitted—from March to June—except for the exempt states of Iowa, New Hampshire, Nevada, and South Carolina. Those contests were held in January, as was the Florida primary, in violation of the rules that had mandated a starting date of February 1 or after for the exempt states. Penalties were imposed by the national Republican party on states that held January and February events, including Florida, New Hampshire, South Carolina, Arizona, and Michigan, but not on the caucus states of Iowa, Nevada, Colorado, Minnesota, and Maine where the results were non-binding.

- For the first time in modern history, corporations and unions are now free to make unlimited expenditures from their general treasuries calling for defeat of specific candidates. In addition to adapting to this new environment, presidential candidates and outside groups must consider the decline of the presidential public financing system. In 2008, Barack Obama became the first person elected President, since public funds were first offered in 1976, who declined to accept

---

[1] 2 U.S.C. §441b(a).

any public funds. It is possible that 2012 will make the first occasion in which neither major-party nominee will accept any public funds.

- Debate over the current relevance of the electoral college has been a recurring theme for decades—a topic that has reemerged ahead of the 2012 election cycle. Despite relative inactivity on the issue in recent years, several states have proposed moving to direct election of the President. The 2012 cycle and related developments may suggest renewed interest in reconsidering presidential selection in the future.

Additional discussion appears throughout this report.

2012: A Reversal of the Front-loading Trend[2]

For the first time in nearly 25 years, the primary and caucus calendar did not feature a crowded series of events in early February or March. As the result of a coordinated effort between Democrats and Republicans at the national level, both parties are expected to enforce a sanctioned "window" for delegate selection events.[3] Democrats first adopted a window in 1980[4] (and effectively exempted Iowa and New Hampshire),[5] but Republicans were unable to garner support for the concept until 2010.[6] Previous attempts by Republicans to do so for the 2004 and 2008 elections were unsuccessful, partly because the party had to approve such changes at the quadrennial national convention, for the following election cycle. In both cases, the plans failed to receive the necessary support within the party to be referred to the national conventions. However, the 2008 national convention did approve a committee—the Temporary Delegate Selection Committee—to review delegate selection procedures and make recommendations to the Republican National Committee (RNC), a first for a party that had traditionally deferred to the state parties on most delegate selection matters.[7]

The Temporary Delegate Selection Committee made several recommendations, of which two were adopted as important amendments to party rules and which have been significant in shaping

---

[2] Kevin J. Coleman (x7-7878), Analyst in Elections, authored this section.

[3] "Thruster v laggards; The 2012 primaries," *The Economist*, April 23, 2011, at http://www.economist.com/node/18587538.

[4] Democratic National Committee, *Delegate Selection Rules for the 1980 Democratic National Convention*, June 9, 1978, Rule 10, p. 10.

[5] Rule 10 of the Democrat's 1980 *Delegate Selection Rules* stated that no first stage determining event could be held "prior to the second Tuesday in March or after the second Tuesday in June" of the election year and noted that "[I]n no instance may a state which scheduled delegate selection procedures on or between the second Tuesday in March and the second Tuesday in June 1976 move out of compliance with the provisions of this rule." The 1976 Iowa caucuses were held on January 19 and the New Hampshire primary was held on February 24. Democrats formalized the exemptions in the 1984 rules by allowing Iowa to hold caucuses 15 days before the second Tuesday in March and New Hampshire to hold its primary 7 days before that date. Democratic National Committee, *Delegate Selection Rules for the 1984 Democratic National Convention*, as adopted by the Democratic National Committee on March 26, 1982, Rule 10, pp. 11-12.

[6] Stuart Rothenberg, "Can Small RNC Rule Change Affect GOP Race?" *Roll Call*, September 8, 2011, at http://www.rollcall.com/issues/57_25/can_small_rnc_rule_change_affect_gop_race-208531-1.html?zkMobileView=true.

[7] Elaine C. Kamarck, *Primary Politics: How Presidential Candidates Have Shaped the Modern Nominating System*, (Washington: Brookings Institution Press, 2009), p. xii.

---

the 2012 primary cycle (see the section entitled "The Outlook for 2012" for a longer discussion of these changes). The first concerned the calendar, and specifically the imposition of a "window" during which primary and caucus events may be held,[8] such as the Democrats have had since 1980. Republicans had never before imposed a timing rule. The change stipulated that no delegate selection event could be held before the first Tuesday in March (March 6, 2012), with exceptions for Iowa, New Hampshire, South Carolina, and Nevada, which can begin the delegate selection process on or after February 1. The window would not apply if Democrats fail to adhere to similar timing.

The second change, also unprecedented for Republicans, required states to use proportional allocation of national convention delegates for any contest held before April 1.[9] Democrats have long mandated proportional allocation of delegates, based on primary and caucus results. The intent was for states that want to retain the preferred winner-take-all system to move the primary or caucus to a date after April 1 to comply, presumably resulting in a less front-loaded calendar as a result. That goal was largely achieved.

The contest began on the same date as in 2008 (January 3), but the slower pace of primaries and caucuses and the use of proportional allocation affected the ability of any of the candidates to close out the race early. By the end of February in 2008, Republican events had already been held in 36 states and the race was announced over shortly thereafter on March 4.[10] In 2012, only 10 such events had been held by the same date. Furthermore, the widespread use of the winner-take-all system for awarding delegates in the past helped the front-runner accumulate a majority of delegates and end the race early. The mandate to use proportional allocation before April 1 (there was a loophole that allowed states to award delegates on a winner-take-all basis if the candidate surpassed 50% in the preference vote) contributed to prolonging the contest, resulting in more primary spending and party infighting. The penalty for violating the proportional allocation rule was not specified in the Republican rules, but guidance provided to the state parties by the RNC stated that "the definition of 'proportional allocation' is left to each state's individual discretion, subject to a final determination in accordance with the rules, " but departing from the requirement for proportional allocation "carries significant risk that not all delegates will be seated."[11] The party did penalize the five states that held binding primaries before March 6, thereby violating the new the timing rule: New Hampshire (January 3), South Carolina (January 21), Florida (January 31), Arizona, and Michigan (February 28). The party reduced each state's national convention delegation by 50%. Iowa and other caucus states that held events ahead of the March 6 start date were not penalized because the results were not binding. Similarly, Missouri's February 7 primary was not binding as well.

---

[8] Republican National Committee, *The Rules of the Republican Party*, As Adopted by the 2008 Republican National Convention, September 1, 2008 (amended August 6, 2010), Rule 15, p. 18.

[9] The significance of the primaries and caucuses is in choosing the delegates to the national party conventions, where the nominees are chosen. Allocating delegates on a proportional basis, based on a candidate's share of the primary or caucus preferences, can yield very different results than using a winner-take-all allocation method.

[10] CNN Politics, "Clinton wins key primaries, CNN projects; McCain clinches nod," March 4, 2008, available at http://articles.cnn.com/2008-03-04/politics/march.4.contests_1_conservative-base-ohio-counties-mike-huckabee?_s= PM:POLITICS.

[11] Republican National Committee, "New Timing Rules for 2012 Republican Presidential Nominating Schedule," memorandum, February 11, 2011, p. 4.

Finally, the calendar and rule changes also led to speculation that no candidate would accumulate a majority of delegates by the end of the primary season, resulting in a brokered convention.[12] Others suggested that only one of the candidates could prevail by the end of the primary season.[13] While there were mixed views about how long the contest would go on and how it would end, many party leaders decried the changes brought about by the new rules and argued that they would damage the nominee in the general election.[14] At the 2012 convention, the party adopted two rules changes that will potentially affect the contest in 2016. The first change will bind delegates to primary and caucus outcomes and was strenuously opposed by supporters of Representative Ron Paul,[15] while the second allows the party to change rules between elections, rather than only at the quadrennial conventions.[16]

The Origins of Front-Loading

Front-loading came about largely because of the prominence of the New Hampshire primary and the Iowa caucuses in the nominating process. The era of rules changes that Democrats initiated after the 1968 convention encouraged state parties to adopt primaries, but the subsequent rise in the number of primaries did not initially result in a more front-loaded calendar. Scattered efforts to schedule early events in other states to attract candidate attention or promote a "native son," either individually or as part of a regional effort, only resulted in Iowa and New Hampshire scheduling even earlier events over time to protect their "first-in-the-nation" status. (The New Hampshire primary was held at the end of February in 1976, 1980, and 1984, and it was last held on January 8 in 2008 and January 10, 2012; the Iowa caucuses were held in late January and February between 1976 and 1984; they were held on January 3 in 2008 and 2012.) In addition to being the first to assess the candidates, the two states benefit economically from hosting the various presidential campaigns in the months before the voting begins. One estimate noted that New Hampshire could reap $264 million because of its early date in 2012.[17]

With a few exceptions, most states did not challenge Iowa and New Hampshire's claim to being first. Democrats continued to revise their rules after each election and the party eventually adopted its current timing rule at the 1980 election, which provided an exemption from the party's sanctioned "window" for delegate selection events for Iowa and New Hampshire.[18]

---

[12] Michael D. Shear, "Santorum Says Romney's Delegate Lead Will Fade as the Contest Continues," *New York Times*, March 13, 2012, p. 14.

[13] Ross Douthat, "The Frontrunner and His Rivals," *The New York Times Blogs*, March 9, 2012.

[14] David M. Drucker, "Senate Republicans Dread Drawn-Out GOP Primary," *Roll Call*, March 14, 2012, at http://www.rollcall.com/issues/57_109/Senate_Republicans_Dread_Long_GOP_Primary-213096-1.html; and Robert Hendin, "Romney backer: Brokered convention would be chaos," CBSNews.com, March 14, 2012, available at http://www.cbsnews.com/8301-3460_162-57397251/romney-backer-brokered-convention-would-be-chaos/.

[15] Stephen Ohlemacher, "Pau's Delegates Defy New GOP Rules to Limit Insurgents," *Star-Ledger*, August 28, 2012, p. 7.

[16] Shannon Tavis, "Rules Fight Sparks Drama at RNC," CNN.com, August 28, 2012, at http://politicalticker.blogs.cnn.com/2012/08/28/rules-fight-sparks-drama-at-rnc/.

[17] Gerald D. Skoning, "Commentary: Why should Iowa and New Hampshire always go first?" *Palm Beach Post*, October 6, 2011, available at http://www.palmbeachpost.com/opinion/commentary/commentary-why-should-iowa-and-new-hampshire-always-1900137.html?printArticle=y.

[18] Ibid., pp. 56-57.

Figure 1. Number of Democratic and Republican Primaries and Caucuses by Month, 1996–2012

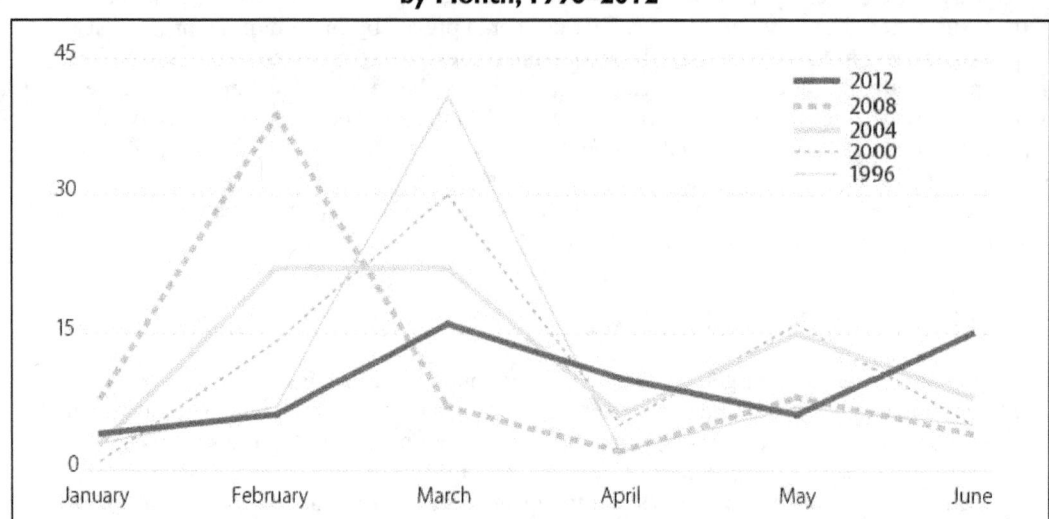

Source: CRS figure based on Federal Election Commission data.

Notes: The data include primaries and caucuses held for one or both parties on a single date.

In 1988, when Iowa voted on February 8 and New Hampshire voted on February 16, the organization of the southern Super Tuesday regional primary on March 8 accelerated the "front-loading" phenomenon. The Super Tuesday event was organized by the Southern Legislative Conference (SLC), a group of southern and border state legislators, and included primaries in 14 states on a single date.[19] It was designed to increase the impact of southern voters in the nominating process and possibly encourage and promote southern candidates who might enter the race. In the presidential election cycles that followed, Iowa and New Hampshire continued to vote in February until the 2000 election, when Iowa held caucuses on January 24 and the New Hampshire primary was on February 1.[20] In the meantime, however, large numbers of states that were not exempt from the Democratic party window began scheduling primaries or caucuses at the beginning of the window, following the Super Tuesday model, and accelerating the nominating season because so many delegates were at stake within the first few weeks of voting. The last primaries traditionally have been held in early June. The front-loading phenomenon meant that clusters of state contests on a single date dominated the early part of the calendar, but the length of the nominating season was not shortened. This, in turn, reinforced the view that the contest was over before voters in later state contests had cast their ballots.

The effort to reduce front-loading for the 2012 election was largely successful, as demonstrated in **Figure 1**. The early part of the calendar is very similar to 2008's, with Iowa on January 3,

---

[19] The Southern Legislative Conference states that held primaries on March 8 included Alabama, Arkansas, Florida, Georgia, Kentucky, Louisiana, Maryland, Mississippi, Missouri, North Carolina, Oklahoma, Tennessee, Texas, and Virginia. In South Carolina, Democrats held caucuses on March 5 and Republicans held a primary on March 12. A precursor southern event took place on March 13, 1984 with primaries in Alabama, Florida and Georgia, in addition to two primaries in the Northeast and Democratic caucuses in four other scattered states.

[20] In the years between 1988 and 2008, various state parties scheduled caucus events in January and February before Iowa or New Hampshire or both, but did not eclipse either state's status in the Presidential nominating season.

followed by New Hampshire (January 10), South Carolina (January 21), and Nevada (February 4). However, while the 2008 calendar featured more February contests than any other month—including 15 primaries and four caucuses for both parties on the first Tuesday—there are only a handful this time, partly because of the new timing rule adopted by both parties that established March as the starting point for nonexempt states. Budget woes caused some states to consolidate the presidential primary with the regular state primary, as California did,[21] while others canceled the presidential primary altogether, as did Utah[22] and Washington.[23] While the 2012 starting date for exempted states was the same as it was in 2008, there were very few contests in February and the bulk of the primaries and caucuses were more-or-less evenly distributed from March to June. The fast pace of early events in 2008 was replaced with a more sequential calendar, but the slower pace resulted in a prolonged contest that was expected to last until June or even remain unresolved until the convention, although that did not come to pass.

Why Do Iowa and New Hampshire Go First?

The New Hampshire primary has been an important event since 1952, when the primary ballot allowed a voter to mark his or her presidential candidate preference for the first time. The preference vote was not connected to the selection of delegates, but the results boosted the candidacies of General Dwight D. Eisenhower and Senator Estes Kefauver at the expense of favorites Senator Robert Taft and President Harry Truman, respectively, and captured the attention of the media because they provided an early gauge of candidate strength or weakness. Although New Hampshire had first adopted its presidential primary in 1913—eventually moved in 1915 to the second Tuesday in March to coincide with town meetings—voters in the primary cast their ballots for unpledged delegates. It rose to prominence because of the preference vote that debuted in 1952.[24] New Hampshire has protected its "first-in-the-nation" primary status by legislating that it is held on the second Tuesday in March, but gives the secretary of state the power to change the date so that it precedes any similar contest by seven days.[25] The national Democratic Party has protected, in effect, New Hampshire's frontrunner primary status since 1980 by restricting the period during which state parties may hold contests (and exempting Iowa and New Hampshire), and the national Republican Party formalized that arrangement as well for the 2012 nominating season.

---

[21] See http://www.sos.ca.gov/elections/elections_cand.htm.

[22] Lisa Riley Roche, "Huntsman, Romney both say they'd be competitive in earlier Utah primary," *Deseret News*, June 28, 2011, at http://www.deseretnews.com/article/705375352/Huntsman-Romney-both-say-they'd-be-competitive-in-earlier-Utah-primary.html.

[23] Washington Secretary of State Sam Reed, "Washington suspends 2012 presidential primary; regular state primary still on," press release, May 12, 2011, at http://www.sos.wa.gov/office/osos_news.aspx?i=zwm8zI6TS07Z8OKbW30dOw%3D%3D.

[24] William G. Mayer, "The New Hampshire Primary: A Historical Overview" in Gary R. Orren and Nelson W. Polsby, eds., *Media and Momentum: The New Hampshire Primary and Nomination Politics* (Chatham, NJ: Chatham House, 1987), pp. 10-11.

[25] The New Hampshire Election Code, Chapter 653:9 states The presidential primary election shall be held on the second Tuesday in March or on a date selected by the secretary of state which is 7 days or more immediately preceding the date on which any other state shall hold a similar election, whichever is earlier, of each year when a president of the United States is to be elected or the year previous. Said primary shall be held in connection with the regular March town meeting or election or, if held on any other day, at a special election called by the secretary of state for that purpose."

New Hampshire voters have successfully picked the eventual party nominees in 8 of 15 Democratic primaries and in 12 of 15 Republican primaries since 1952, including 11 from both parties who were elected or reelected President (see **Table 1**). Criticism of New Hampshire's status and influence, however, has been virtually unrelenting in the intervening decades. Given its small size, the state receives media attention that is disproportionate. Between 1988 and 1996, New Hampshire received between 17% and 23% of all television coverage during the nomination phase.[26] In comparison, the California primary garnered 5% of media coverage in 1996, *after* the primary was moved up to March from its usual June date. Aside from the obvious benefits of having a monopoly on being the first primary (the Iowa caucuses are earlier), the New Hampshire primary has been criticized not only because of the small number of participants who wield such influence in the first stage of the presidential election, but also because the state is not representative of the country's demographics (see **Table 2**).

Table 1. New Hampshire Primary Winners Since 1952

Year	Democrats		Republicans	
	Primary Winner	**Nominee**	**Primary Winner**	**Nominee**
1952	Estes Kefauver	Adlai E. Stevenson	**Dwight D. Eisenhower**	**Dwight D. Eisenhower**
1956	Estes Kefauver	Adlai E. Stevenson	**Dwight D. Eisenhower**	**Dwight D. Eisenhower**
1960	**John F. Kennedy**	**John F. Kennedy**	Richard M. Nixon	Richard M. Nixon
1964	**Lyndon B. Johnson**	**Lyndon B. Johnson**	Henry Cabot Lodge	Barry Goldwater
1968	Lyndon B. Johnson	Hubert H. Humphrey	**Richard M. Nixon**	**Richard M. Nixon**
1972	Edmund S. Muskie	George McGovern	**Richard M. Nixon**	**Richard M. Nixon**
1976	**James E. Carter**	**James E. Carter**	Gerald R. Ford	Gerald R. Ford
1980	James E. Carter	James E. Carter	**Ronald Reagan**	**Ronald Reagan**
1984	Gary Hart	Walter F. Mondale	**Ronald Reagan**	**Ronald Reagan**
1988	Michael S. Dukakis	Michael S. Dukakis	**George H.W. Bush**	**George H.W. Bush**
1992	Paul E. Tsongas	**William J. Clinton**	George Bush	George Bush
1996	**William J. Clinton**	**William J. Clinton**	Patrick J. Buchanan	Robert J. Dole
2000	Albert Gore, Jr.	Albert Gore, Jr.	John McCain	**George W. Bush**
2004	John F. Kerry	John F. Kerry	**George W. Bush**	**George W. Bush**
2008	Hillary Rodham Clinton	**Barack H. Obama**	John S. McCain	John S. McCain
2012	Barack H. Obama	Barack H. Obama	Willard Mitt Romney	Willard Mitt Romney

Source: *Guide to U.S. Elections*, (Washington: CQ Press, 2005), various pages and, for 2008, the New Hampshire Secretary of State website, at http://www.sos.nh.gov/presprim2008/index.htm.

Notes: Candidate names in bold indicate those who were elected or reelected President.

---

[26] Harold W. Stanley and Richard G. Niemi, *Vital Statistics on American Politics, 2001-2002*, (Washington: CQ Press, 2001), pp. 178-179.

The Iowa caucuses rose to prominence largely as the result of events in 1972, when Democrats first held their caucuses in January (Republican caucuses were in April). Democrats were operating under entirely new nominating rules designed to democratize the delegate selection process. The reforms had been implemented as a result of the violence and upheaval at the 1968 Democratic National Convention in Chicago, based on subsequent recommendations from the party's Commission on Party Structure and Delegate Selection,[27] also known as the McGovern/Fraser Commission. Iowa was the first event of the nominating season under the new rules. Although the results of the January 24 precinct caucuses were imprecise, presumed frontrunner Senator Edmund Muskie was unexpectedly challenged by Senator George McGovern (of the McGovern/Fraser Commission), who finished third behind Muskie. "Uncommitted" was first. Although Muskie was the leading candidate in Iowa, his campaign had performed below so-called media expectations, to some extent, which damaged his frontrunner status. For his part, McGovern had recognized both the importance of the new rules and Iowa's January 24 caucuses and had begun organizing in the state months before other candidates.[28] A closer than expected result in the New Hampshire primary that followed on March 7, which Muskie won with McGovern second, further slowed Muskie's campaign.[29] McGovern eventually prevailed in winning the nomination, only to lose badly to President Richard Nixon in the general election (520 to 17 in the electoral college).

Table 2. Comparative Demographic Data for the United States and Early Primary and Caucus States

	United States	New Hampshire	Iowa	South Carolina	Nevada
Population	308,745,538	1,316,470	3,046,355	4,625,364	2,700,551
White	72.4%	93.9%	91.3%	66.2%	66.2%
Black	12.6%	1.1%	2.9%	27.9%	8.1%
Hispanic	16.3%	2.8%	5.0%	5.1%	26.5%
Asian	4.8%	2.2%	1.7%	1.3%	7.2%
Union membership	10.9%	10.2%	11.4%	4.6%	15%

Source: U.S. Census Bureau, "State & County Quick Facts," http://quickfacts.census.gov/qfd/states/32000.html and the AFL-CIO, "Union Members by State, 2010," http://www.aflcio.org/joinaunion/why/uniondifference/uniondiff16.cfm.

The 1972 Democratic caucuses had alerted the media to the pitfalls of misinterpreting pre-election year expectations and to the practical usefulness of Iowa's early caucus results. When Republicans joined Democrats in setting a date for the 1976 caucuses on January 18, Iowa was positioned to leverage its status as the first contest of the nominating season. Governor James E. Carter scored a surprise victory in Iowa after extensive campaigning there and he was rewarded with a windfall of press coverage. He further boosted his momentum with a win in New Hampshire five weeks later. On the Republican side, President Gerald R. Ford narrowly defeated

---

[27] Democratic National Committee, "Mandate for Reform: A Report of the Commission on Party Structure and Delegate Selection to the Democratic National Committee," April, 1970.

[28] Hugh Winebrenner, *The Iowa Precinct Caucuses: The Making of a Media Event* (Ames: Iowa University Press, 1987), pp. 53-64.

[29] Bill Kovach, "Balloting Heavy," *New York Times*, March 8, 1972, p. 1.

Governor Ronald Reagan in a straw poll that was unrelated to the selection of delegates, but which also fueled post-caucus coverage of the event. In the end, the cooperation of the parties to extensively promote the Iowa caucuses in 1976 was successful and a second small, unrepresentative state became a starting place for the presidential nominating season.

Two additional states were given exemptions in 2008 to the Democrats' timing rules. South Carolina and Nevada were added because they were demographically more representative of the nation—and particularly of elements in the Democratic party base—than New Hampshire and Iowa.[30] Nevada has a large union presence and Hispanic population, and South Carolina has a substantial black population.

Democratic vs. Republican Delegate Selection Rules

The two national parties are a study in contrasts with regard to the rules for nominating presidential candidates. The Democrats engineered the wholesale revision of the process in 1970 in the name of "democratization," and some of those changes were enacted by state legislatures in the years that followed. Democratic party rules are numerous, detailed, and administered at the national level. Republicans have fewer rules and the national party has mostly deferred to the state parties on how the delegates are selected. There are some similarities, however. Both parties allocate delegates to the states on a congressional district and statewide (at-large) basis, as well as allocating additional "bonus" delegates according to the strength of the Democratic or Republican party vote for certain offices in previous elections. Each party also assigns automatic delegates to the states for party or elected officials, although Democrats have many more such delegates (referred to in the press as "superdelegates"). Both parties use the primary and caucus process, or a combination of the two, to select delegates. And finally, both parties convene a national convention in August or September to select the presidential and vice presidential nominees (the party that controls the White House usually convenes its convention last). In 2012, Republicans met in Tampa, FL, from August 27-30 and Democrats met in Charlotte, NC, from September 3-6. The Republican convention initially appeared to be in the path of Hurricane Isaac, but the storm veered west into the Gulf of Mexico. RNC Chairman Reince Priebus opened the convention on Monday, August 27, and put it in recess within a minute.[31] The convention resumed on Tuesday, August 28.

As for the differences between the parties on delegate selection, there are many. Democrats seek to encourage the participation and representation of groups that have been "explicitly denied the right to vote or have been subjected to discriminatory and exclusionary practices."[32] The national party imposes affirmative action goals to achieve participation by these groups according to their presence in the electorate, but does not allow the use of quotas. The rules instruct states to give priority consideration to African Americans, Hispanics, Native Americans, Asian Americans and Pacific Islanders, and women in selecting at-large delegates and alternates, if needed, to fulfill the affirmative action goals outlined in the state's delegate selection plan. State delegations are also

---

[30] Chris Cillizza and Zachary A. Goldfarb, "Democrats Tweak the Primary Calendar," *Washington Post*, July 23, 2006, A 4.

[31] Alessandra Stanley, "Convention Postponed, But the Show Must Go On," *New York Times*, August 28, 2012, Section A, p. 13.

[32] Rule 6 (A), Democratic National Committee, *Delegate Selection Rules for the 2012 Democratic National Convention*, issued by the Democratic Party of the United States (recommended for adoption by the full DNC at its meeting August 20, 2010), p. 6.

required to provide for equal numbers of men and women delegates and alternates in the state delegation and at the district level as well, if possible. The party also seeks to include LGBT (lesbian, gay, bisexual, and transgender) individuals, people with disabilities, and youth in the delegate selection process, and party affairs generally, according to their presence in the Democratic electorate.[33] The Republican Party does not impose affirmative action goals for the state parties, but notes that

> participation in a Republican primary, caucus, or any meeting or convention ... shall in no way be abridged for reasons of sex, race, religion, color, age, or national origin. The Republican National Committee and the state Republican party or governing committee of each state shall take positive action to achieve the broadest possible participation by men and women, young people, minority and heritage groups, senior citizens, and all other citizens in the delegate election, selection, allocation, or binding process.[34]

The Republican rules also note that "each state shall endeavor to have equal representation of men and women in its delegation" to the convention.[35]

Voter participation in primaries and caucuses is controlled by national party rules, state laws, and state party rules. This overlapping authority is largely the result of state laws concerning open and closed primaries and the national parties' efforts to restrict participation to those who are either registered with the party or aligned with its principles. Restricting participation to "party voters" is complicated by uneven state voter registration procedures under which a voter may not be required to declare a party. At the national level, Republicans limit participation to "persons eligible to vote who are deemed as a matter of public record to be Republicans pursuant to state law or, if voters are not enrolled by party, by Republican party rules of a state."[36] Two other provisions note that "the applicable Republican party rules of a state may prescribe additional qualifications not inconsistent with state law" and that "no state law shall be observed that permits any person to participate in a primary ... that also permits that person at the same primary to participate in the choosing of nominees of any other party."[37] Comparable Democratic party rules note that "[p]articipation in the delegate selection process shall be open to all voters who wish to participate as Democrats" and that "Democratic voters shall be those persons who publicly declare their Party preference and have that preference publicly recorded."[38] With respect to closed primary states, the Democratic party rules note that "nothing in these rules shall be interpreted to encourage or permit states with party registration and enrollment ... to amend their systems to open participation to members of other parties."[39] And, finally, the rules say that state parties should "encourage nonaffiliated and new voters to register or enroll" with the party and

---

[33] Rule 7, Democratic National Committee, *Delegate Selection Rules for the 2012 Democratic National Convention*, issued by the Democratic Party of the United States (recommended for adoption by the full DNC at its meeting August 20, 2010), p. 8.

[34] Rule 4 (a), Republican National Committee, *The Rules of the Republican Party*, as adopted by the 2008 Republican National Convention, September 1, 2008, and amended by the Republican National Committee on August 6, 2010, p. 17.

[35] Ibid., Rule 4 (d).

[36] Ibid., Rule 15 (c)(2).

[37] Ibid., Rule 15 (c)(2) and (c)(3).

[38] Rule 2 (A) and 2 (A)(1), Democratic National Committee, *Delegate Selection Rules for the 2012 Democratic National Convention*, issued by the Democratic Party of the United States (recommended for adoption by the full DNC at its meeting August 20, 2010), p. 2.

[39] Ibid., Rule 2 (B).

that "no person shall participate or vote in the nominating process for a Democratic presidential candidate who also participates in the nominating processes of any other party for corresponding elections."[40]

The parties' methods of allocating delegate and alternate slots to the states and territories vary considerably, as do the rules for conducting primaries and caucuses and awarding delegates based on the results.

In a reversal of their usual positions, the Democratic party rule on binding delegates is much simpler than Republican rules. The rule says simply that "[d]elegates elected to the national convention pledged to a presidential candidate shall in all good conscience reflect the sentiments of those who elected them."[41] Republicans do not have a national party rule on whether delegates are bound or not, and defer to the state parties on the matter. As a result, there is a great deal of variety among the state delegations at the convention with respect to how delegates may cast their votes.

Delegate selection procedures are based on a number of documents. For Democrats, the documents include the *Call for the 2012 Democratic National Convention*, the *Rules and Bylaws of the National Democratic Party*, and, most importantly, the *Delegate Selection Rules For the 2012 Democratic National Convention*. For Republicans, the *Rules of the Republican Party* and the *Call of the 2012 Convention* control the delegate selection process. The number of delegates to the 2012 Democratic National Convention was 5,077 (and 371 alternates)[42] and the number of delegates to the Republican National Convention was 2,286 (and 2,119 alternates). State Democratic parties were required to submit delegate selection plans to the national party for approval by the Rules and Bylaws Committee: "State Delegate Selection Plans, Affirmative Action Plans and Inclusion Programs shall be submitted to the DNC Rules and Bylaws Committee for approval on or before May 2, 2011."[43]

Types of Delegates

The methods the parties use to allocate delegates (and alternates) to each of the states and the territories are characteristically different. Democrats have two categories of delegates, pledged and unpledged, according to whether or not the delegates are required to express a presidential candidate or uncommitted preference as a condition of election (as shown in **Table 3**). Pledged district delegates are allocated and elected at a district level (usually the congressional district, but sometimes by state legislative district), and at-large delegates are allocated and elected at the statewide level. Both of these types of delegates are allocated to each state according to a formula called the "allocation factor" (discussed in greater detail below). A third type of pledged delegate is called an "Add-on" delegate, that allows for representation by party leaders and elected officials within the state. The number of such delegates is calculated by multiplying the number of total base delegates for a state by 15%, so it is also based on the allocation factor.

---

[40] Ibid., Rule 2 (E).

[41] Ibid., Rule 12 (J).

[42] Democratic Party of the United States, *Call For the 2012 Democratic National Convention*, as adopted by the Democratic Party of the United States, August 20, 2010, p. 31.

[43] Rule 1 (D), Democratic National Committee, *Delegate Selection Rules for the 2012 Democratic National Convention*, p. 2

Table 3. Types of Democratic Party Delegates, 2012

	Pledged Total Base Delegates 3,792			Unpledged ("Superdelegates") 721			
District	At-Large	Add-On	DNC Members	Members of Congress	Governors	Distinguished Party Leaders	Total
2,819	973	564	436	240	20	25	5,087

Source: Democratic National Committee, *Call for the 2012 Democratic National Convention*, as adopted on August 20, 2010, p. 31.

Democrats begin the allocation process with a base of 3,700 delegate votes, which are assigned to the states and the District of Columbia based on the allocation factor. The allocation factor is a formula that relies on the state's Democratic vote in the previous three presidential elections and the assigned number of electoral college votes, divided by the corresponding national totals, to assign the delegates. The formula is expressed as follows:

$$A= \frac{1}{2}\left(\frac{SDV\,2000 + SDV\,2004 + SDV\,2008}{TDV\,2000 + TDV\,2004 + TDV\,2008} + \frac{SEV}{538}\right)$$

A = allocation factor

SDV = state vote for Democratic candidate in the year indicated

TDV = total vote for Democratic candidate in the year indicated

SEV = state electoral college vote

For example, South Dakota's allocation factor is .004012, so its base number of delegates is: .004012 x 3,700 = 14.85, or 15 delegates. The base delegates are assigned as district level delegates (75% of the base, or 11 delegates) and at-large delegates (25% of the base, or 4 delegates). South Dakota is also entitled to two add-on delegate slots for party leaders and elected officials in the state. Delegates in these three categories are pledged delegates and required to express a presidential candidate or uncommitted preference as a condition of election. The state is also allocated a number of unpledged delegates, including five for its members of the Democratic National Committee, one for its Democratic Member of Congress, and one for the former Senate majority leader as a Distinguished Party Leader delegate. These are the superdelegates (discussed in greater detail in the next section). Thus, the total number of delegates for South Dakota is 24, with 2 alternates, for a total delegation of 26. One alternate is allotted for every 12 convention votes.

Democrats also allocate delegates for five entities for which the allocation factor cannot be computed because they do not participate in presidential elections: American Samoa, Democrats Abroad, Guam, Puerto Rico, and the Virgin Islands. The party assigns at-large delegates to each entity, which also receives delegate slots for its members of the DNC, Members of Congress, and Democratic governors.

Republicans use a simpler delegate allocation method than the Democrats. The party assigns 10 at large delegates to each state, as well as 3 delegates per congressional district. In addition, the party assigns bonus delegates to a state that cast its electoral votes (or a majority thereof) for the Republican nominee in the preceding election, and also assigns a single at-large delegate to states in which Republicans were elected to the following: the governor's office, at least one half of the seats in the U.S. House of Representatives, a majority of the members of a chamber of the state legislature (if the presiding officer is a Republican elected by the chamber), a majority of members in all chambers of a state legislature (if the presiding officers are Republicans elected by each chamber), or a U.S. Senate seat (in the six-year period preceding the presidential election year). Republicans assign one alternate for each delegate.

Republicans assign at-large delegates to the District of Columbia, Guam, the Northern Mariana Islands, Puerto Rico and the Virgin Islands. The District of Columbia is also eligible for bonus delegates if it cast its electoral vote (or a majority thereof) for the Republican nominee in the preceding election.

Superdelegates

Another difference between the parties is the number of automatic delegate slots each party reserves for party or elected officials. Although the Republican Party designates as automatic delegates the three members of the Republican National Committee from each state, the term "superdelegate" has generally been used in reference to a group of unpledged Democratic Party delegates.[44] These delegates are designated automatically and are not required to make known their presidential candidate or uncommitted preference, in contrast to all the other elected delegates. They include all Democratic Party Members of Congress and governors; members of the Democratic National Committee; distinguished party members who include former Presidents and Vice Presidents, former Democratic leaders of the Senate, Speakers of the House, and minority leaders; and former chairs of the Democratic National Committee. The superdelegates were added after the 1980 election when incumbent President James E. Carter lost to Governor Ronald Reagan in a 489-49 electoral vote landslide. The belief was that superdelegates, as party and elected leaders, could serve as a counterweight to rank and file party voters in evaluating presidential candidates.[45] In this way, the superdelegates represented an effort to somewhat reverse the effect of the 1970s reforms that diminished the influence of "party elders." Democrats increased the number of such delegates every four years since they were introduced in 1984 until the 2012 convention, for which they were slightly reduced.[46] For Republicans, the automatic delegates to the convention made up slightly less than 7% of the national convention.

---

[44] In the 2012 election cycle, the media now routinely refers to the RNC delegates to the convention as superdelegates.

[45] William G. Mayer, *In Pursuit of the White House: How We Choose Our Presidential Nominees*, (Chatham, NJ: Chatham House Publishers, Inc., 1996), pp. 123-124.

[46] Democrats eliminated one category of superdelegates that are "add-on" slots for state and local party and elected officials.

Figure 2. Democratic Party Delegates, 2012

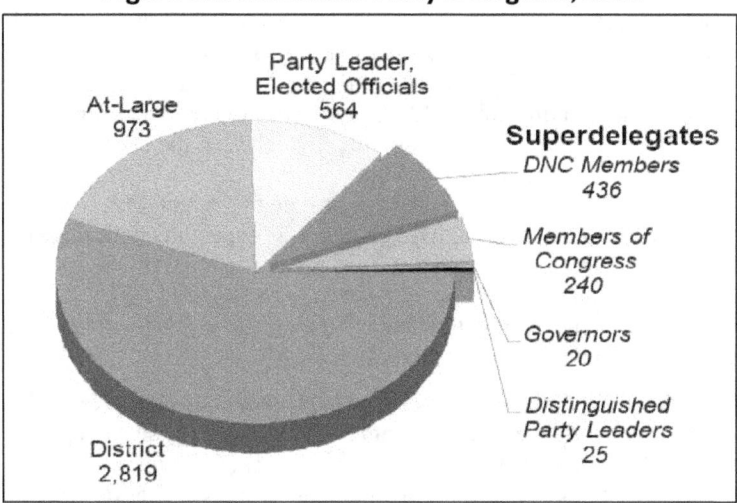

Source: CRS figure based on Democratic Party of the United States, *Call for the 2012 Democratic National Convention*, August 20, 2010, Appendix B.

Notes: Delegate totals are subject to change because of interim election results, resignations, and deaths.

For most of their existence, the superdelegates attracted little attention,[47] but in 2008, it appeared that they might decide the contest. By February, Senator Hillary Clinton and Senator Barack Obama were so evenly matched in the fight to win delegates that the campaigns courted individually many of the 796 superdelegates, who were nearly 20% of the convention total.[48] The contest was not resolved until the last events on the calendar, the June 3 primaries in South Dakota and Montana. Obama claimed victory with 1,763 pledged and 438 superdelegates (2,201), as compared to 1,640 pledged and 256 superdelegates for Clinton (1,896). A candidate needed 2,118 to win the nomination.

The Outlook for 2012

The delegate selection process in any given election year is usually shaped by events that occurred in the previous cycle. That was especially true for the 2012 nominating season.

- Because of the front-loading that again characterized the calendar in 2008, Democrats and Republicans for the first time agreed upon a plan to control the calendar with a window for delegate selection events, that begins on March 6, 2012, for all but the exempt states of Iowa, New Hampshire, Nevada, and South Carolina. The inter-party cooperation was unprecedented, as was the adoption of a new Republican party rule, also intended to reduce front-loading, that required the use of proportional allocation to divide delegates in contests held before April

---

[47] Vice President Walter Mondale needed 323 (out of 1,937) superdelegates to claim the nomination over Senator Gary Hart in 1984. Mondale declared victory on the date of the last primaries, June 5, but would not have had a majority without the superdelegates, a fact that was largely obscured because of the timing of his victory announcement. Elaine C. Kamarck, *Primary Politics: How Presidential Candidates Have Shaped the Modern Nominating System* (Washington: Brookings Institution Press, 2009), pp. 158-160.

[48] Julie Bosman, "Wooing With Charm and PACS," *New York Times*, February 15, 2008, p. 19.

1 (except for the exempted states). Although the party did not specifically define proportional allocation and instead left it to the discretion of the state parties, it marked a change from awarding delegates largely on a winner-take-all basis at any point in the calendar. The new rule introduced an element of uncertainty into the Republican nominating contest. Although the intention was to spread out the contests, in an effort to reverse front-loading by delaying the use of winner-take-all, the result was that it prolonged the nominating battle. Before the contest began, *Roll Call* had reported that the earliest date that a candidate could secure a majority of delegates was April 24.[49] The race was expected to continue long after that date and perhaps until the national convention under the new rules; Governor Romney ultimately claimed the nomination on May 29.[50] In the meantime, without a contest on the Democratic side, the President was free essentially to campaign for the general election.

- The 2012 calendar was finalized on November 2, when the New Hampshire secretary of state announced that the primary would be held on January 10.[51] That announcement was preceded by several months of calendar maneuvering on the part of certain states that began with an announcement that Florida would hold its primary on January 31, 2011. The race began on the same date as in 2008—with the January 3 Iowa caucuses—but it was less front-loaded than it had been in some time. The New Hampshire, South Carolina, and Nevada contests were on virtually the same January dates as in 2008,[52] as was Florida's primary, which violated both parties' rules for 2012. The schedule of contests in February looked quite different than it did in 2008, however, as the first Tuesday featured events in 22 states in that year, whereas only a handful of states (mostly Republican events, except for the Missouri primary) violated party rules to hold February events in 2012. The first Tuesday in March was the officially sanctioned opening date for nonexempt states to hold contests. The January start, followed by a light schedule of events in February represented a dramatic shift in the early characteristics of the calendar in comparison to 2008. Another trend was that a number of states that had early primaries in 2008 moved the contests to later in the year for 2012, such as California and New Jersey (June 5); Ohio (June 12); and Connecticut, Delaware, and New York (April 24). The Democratic contest in 2008 extended into June under a much more front-loaded calendar (albeit with different candidates and dynamics), while many more delegates were at stake in June 2012.

- For many presidential election cycles since 1972, the "law of unintended consequences" has been invoked to explain unwelcome results that sometimes followed from Democratic rules changes. In 2012, with an open nominating

---

[49] Shira Toeplitz, *Roll Call*, "Prolonged 2012 Primary Risky for GOP," December 20, at http://www.rollcall.com/issues/57_77/Prolonged-2012-Primary-Risky-for-GOP-211200-1.html?pos=htmbtxt.

[50] Eric Golub, "Romney Wins Texas, Clinches GOP Nomination; Texas Congressman Soundly Rejected, Returned to Obscurity," *The Washington Times*, May 30, 2012, at http://communities.washingtontimes.com/neighborhood/tygrrrr-express/2012/may/29/romney-wins-texas-clinches-gop-nomination-texas-co/.

[51] Michael D. Shear, *New York Times*, "New Hampshire Claims Its Usual Spot on the Republican Primary Calendar," November 3, 2011, p. 22.

[52] The dates of the Iowa, New Hampshire, South Carolina and Nevada events violate both the DNC and RNC rules for 2012, which provide for these contests to be held in February.

---

contest and unprecedented changes to the rules and calendar, it seemed to be the Republicans who were contending with unintended consequences. As Democrats have done many times in the past, Republicans may be compelled to consider changes to the delegate selection process. To that end, the party approved a rules change at the convention that will allow it to make interim revisions to delegate selection rules before the next nomination contest begins.

Aside from the rules and calendar under which the presidential candidates will compete, the amount of money to be spent in both the primary and general elections phases outpaced that of previous election cycles. New fundraising and spending trends in 2008, and significant changes to campaign finance law since then, suggest that the terrain of the 2012 election is likely to be different than in any election that has preceded it.

Campaign Finance in Presidential Elections[53]

Campaigning for the presidency requires more money today than ever before.[54] Raising funds increasingly requires highly professional campaign staffs, typically supplemented with fundraising consultants and assistance—where permissible—from national party committees.[55] The money raised is spent on every facet of the campaign, particularly political advertising, which is typically a national campaign's largest budget item.[56] Purchasing broadcast airtime to run political ads is especially expensive in major media markets. Even without high airtime costs, the advertising must be produced (usually through the services of professional media consultants), polls must be commissioned to track the campaign's popularity and messages, and all sorts of everyday operational costs must be met.

Federal election law and regulation, discussed below, set the boundaries for how presidential campaigns and other "political committees" (which include candidate committees, party committees, and political action committees [PACs]) raise and spend money. Although public financing dominated presidential campaigns between the 1970s and early 2000s, a combination of legal and strategic developments has increased the emphasis on private money in recent election cycles. The 2012 cycle marked the first since the public financing program's inception in the 1970s that no major candidate accepted public funds. In addition to the amounts raised and spent by candidate campaigns, other entities—especially parties, PACs, and interest groups (e.g., tax-exempt 501(c) and 527 organizations)—are major sources of political funds.

As **Table 4** shows, for the 2012 election cycle, an individual could contribute up to $5,000 to a presidential campaign. Of that amount, $2,500 could be contributed during the primary election. Another $2,500 could be contributed during the general election. Also as the table shows, PACs and parties can contribute to campaigns, just as a presidential campaign could choose to

---

[53] R. Sam Garrett (x7-6443), Specialist in American National Government, authored this section.

[54] For an overview of the changes in funding since the 1970s, see Candice J. Nelson, *Grant Park: The Democratization of Presidential Elections, 1968-2008* (Washington: Brookings Institution Press, 2011), pp. 9-24.

[55] See, for example, R. Sam Garrett, *Campaign Crises: Detours on the Road to Congress* (Boulder, CO: Lynne Rienner Publishers, 2010); and Dennis W. Johnson, *No Place for Amateurs: How Political Consultants are Reshaping American Democracy*, 2nd ed. (New York: Routledge, 2007). Although some of the citations provided in this section are from sources that emphasize congressional campaigns, the concepts also apply to presidential campaigns.

[56] See, for example, John Sides et al., *Campaigns and Elections: Rules, Reality, Strategy, Choice* (New York: W.W. Norton, 2011), p. 264.

---

contribute funds to one of those entities. Importantly, and as discussed below, publicly financed candidates may not accept private contributions in the general election. The limits below also do not necessarily apply to contributions to groups making only independent expenditures—messages that explicitly call for election or defeat of a candidate but which are not coordinated with the campaign.

Table 4. Federal Contribution Limits, 2011–2012

(additional limits appear in the table notes)

Contributor	Recipient			
	Principal campaign committee	**Multicandidate Committee (most PACs, including leadership PACs)**	**National Party Committee (DSCC, NRCC, etc.)**	**State, District, Local Party Committee**
Individual	$2,500 per election*	$5,000 per year	$30,800 per year*	$10,000 per year (combined limit)
Principal Campaign Committee	$2,000 per election	$5,000 per year	Unlimited transfers to party committees	Unlimited transfers to party committees
Multicandidate Committee (most PACs, including leadership PACs)ᵃ	$5,000 per election	$5,000 per year	$15,000 per year	$5,000 per year (combined limit)
State, District, Local Party Committee	$5,000 per election (combined limit)	$5,000 per year (combined limit)	Unlimited transfers to party committees	Unlimited transfers to party committees
National Party Committee	$5,000 per election	$5,000 per year	Unlimited transfers to party committees	Unlimited transfers to party committees

Source: CRS adaptation from FEC, "Contribution Limits for 2011-2012," http://www.fec.gov/info/contriblimits1112.pdf.

Notes: A presidential campaign committee (e.g., Jones for President) is a "principal campaign committee." The same is true for a House or Senate campaign. The table assumes that leadership PACs would qualify for multicandidate status. The original source, noted above, includes additional information and addresses non-multicandidate PACs (which are relatively rare). Limits marked with an asterisk (*) are adjusted biennially for inflation. The table does not include the following notes regarding additional limitations: (1) For individuals, a special biennial limit of $117,000 ($46,200 to all candidate committees and $70,800 to party and PAC committees) also applies. These amounts are adjusted biennially for inflation; (2) Contributions to independent-expenditure-only PACs (super PACs) are unlimited, as are contributions to nonconnected PACs making independent expenditures consistent with the *Carey* decision; (3) The national party committee and the national party Senate committee (e.g., the DNC and DSCC or RNC and NRSC) share a combined per-campaign limit of $43,100, which is adjusted biennially for inflation.

a. "Multicandidate committees" are those that have been registered with the FEC (or, for Senate committees, the Secretary of the Senate) for at least six months; have received federal contributions from more than 50 people; and (except for state parties) have made contributions to at least five federal candidates. See 11 C.F.R. §100.5(e)(3). In practice, most PACs attain this status automatically over time.

Campaign finance in presidential elections has been the subject of extensive research[57] and is governed by complex requirements specified in the Federal Election Campaign Act (FECA), the Internal Revenue Code (IRC), and Federal Election Commission (FEC) regulations.[58] In-depth treatment of these subjects is beyond the scope of this report, which is designed to provide an overview of major issues. The following pages discuss some of the most notable contemporary issues affecting campaign finance in presidential elections. In particular, the discussion includes recent changes in the legal and regulatory environment per the 2010 Supreme Court ruling in *Citizens United v. Federal Election Commission*; the public financing program; and fundraising and spending by campaigns and groups in 2008 and beyond. Among others, key points include the following:

- Major legal changes resulted from the Supreme Court's 2010 *Citizens United* ruling. Although corporations and unions remain prohibited from using their treasury funds to contribute to candidates, the 2012 election cycle was the first in which they could directly (but independently) spend treasury funds to advocate election or defeat of a presidential candidate.

- In 2012, presidential campaigns (like all other federal candidate campaigns) could raise no more than $5,000 from individual contributors ($2,500 for the primary election; $2,500 for the general election).

- Presidential campaigns are on pace to raise record amounts in 2012, in addition to substantial financial activity from parties, political action committees (PACs), and outside groups.

- Although candidates from both parties widely participated in public financing before 2000, the program's popularity has declined in the past decade. In 2008 Barack Obama accepted no public funds. He was the first candidate elected President solely with private funds since public financing was first offered in 1976.

- The decline of public financing is perhaps the greatest change in presidential campaign finance in the past 20 years. No major candidate accepted public funds in 2012.

- Democratic and Republican convention committees received base public financing grants of approximately $18.2 million each.

---

[57] To cite just a few examples, see Herbert E. Alexander, *Financing the 1960 Election* (Princeton, N.J.: Citizens' Research Foundation, 1962) (and subsequent volumes in the series); Raymond J. La Raja, *Small Change: Money, Political Parties, and Campaign Finance Reform* (Ann Arbor: University of Michigan Press, 2008); Costas Panagoupolos and Daniel Bergen, "Contributions and Contributors in the 2004 Presidential Election Cycle," *Presidential Studies Quarterly*, vol. 36, no. 2 (June 2006), pp. 155-171; and *Financing the 2008 Elections: Assessing Reform*, ed. David B. Magleby and Anthony Corrado (Brookings Institution Press, 2011). See also other sources cited throughout this section.

[58] FECA, as amended, is found at 2 U.S.C. §431 *et seq*. Chapters 95 and 96 of the IRC, found in Title 26 of the U.S. Code, are particularly relevant. FEC regulations are found in chapter 11 of the C.F.R.

Recent Major Changes in Campaign Finance Law

Fundraising and spending in federal elections is governed by federal election law and FEC regulations. Other CRS products discuss these topics in detail.[59] In brief:

- Congress established modern campaign finance law in the 1970s by enacting and amending FECA, which emphasized contribution limits, reporting (disclosure) requirements, and establishing the FEC. Parts of FECA, particularly campaign spending limits, were invalidated in the U.S. Supreme Court's landmark *Buckley v. Valeo* decision (1976).[60]

- FECA remained largely unchanged until 2002, when Congress amended the act through the Bipartisan Campaign Reform Act (BCRA), also known as "McCain-Feingold." Among other points, BCRA banned national parties, federal candidates, and officeholders from raising soft money in federal elections; increased most contribution limits; and placed additional restrictions on pre-election issue advocacy. Specifically, the act's electioneering communications provision prohibited corporations and unions from using their treasury funds to air broadcast ads referring to clearly identified federal candidates within 60 days of a general election or 30 days of a primary election or caucus.

- Most notably for recent campaigns and the 2012 presidential election cycle, the U.S. Supreme Court reached another landmark decision in January 2010.[61] In *Citizens United v. Federal Election Commission*, the Court invalidated FECA's prohibitions on corporate and union treasury funding of independent expenditures and electioneering communications. As a consequence of *Citizens United*, corporations and unions are now free to use their treasury funds to air political advertisements explicitly calling for election or defeat of federal or state candidates (independent expenditures) or advertisements that refer to those candidates during pre-election periods, but do not necessarily explicitly call for their election or defeat (electioneering communications). Previously, such advertising would generally have had to be financed through voluntary contributions raised by PACs affiliated with unions or corporations.

- Subsequent litigation and FEC advisory opinions consistent with *Citizens United* and the related case *SpeechNow v. FEC* gave rise to a new form of PAC, known as "super PACs." First active in 2010, super PACs may raise unlimited funds—including from corporations or unions—to air independent expenditures (IEs) or electioneering communications (ECs).

- In October 2011 the FEC announced that, in response to an agreement reached in a case brought after *SpeechNow* (*Carey v. FEC*[62]), the agency would permit

---

[59] See CRS Report R41542, *The State of Campaign Finance Policy: Recent Developments and Issues for Congress*, by R. Sam Garrett; and CRS Report RL30669, *The Constitutionality of Campaign Finance Regulation: Buckley v. Valeo and Its Supreme Court Progeny*, by L. Paige Whitaker.

[60] 424 U.S. 1 (1976).

[61] 130 S. Ct. 876 (2010). For a legal analysis of the case, see CRS Report R41045, *The Constitutionality of Regulating Corporate Expenditures: A Brief Analysis of the Supreme Court Ruling in Citizens United v. FEC*, by L. Paige Whitaker.

[62] Civ. No. 11-259-RMC (D.D.C. 2011).

entities known as "nonconnected" PACs—those that are unaffiliated with corporations or unions—to accept unlimited contributions for use in IEs. These entities are not super PACs, although their behavior might resemble that of super PACs. As of this writing, fewer than 25 nonconnected PACs have indicated they plan to spend funds consistent with the *Carey* agreement.

Transitioning from Public Funds to Private Funds in Recent Election Cycles

Between 1976 and 2000, presidential campaigns were financed almost exclusively with public funds. During this time—the heyday of the presidential public financing program to date—private fundraising was generally perceived to be no match for the comparatively large matching funds and grants taxpayer-funds provided presidential candidates through the public financing program. This was true for both Democratic and Republican candidates.[63] Although Republican candidates are typically philosophically opposed to some campaign finance regulation and taxpayer funding of elections, Republican presidential candidates—like their Democratic counterparts—have actively participated in the public financing program. In fact, between 1976 (the first election cycle in which public financing was offered) and 1996, every major-party nominee accepted public funds in the primary- and general-election campaigns.

Beginning in the late 1990s and early 2000s, however, the public financing program began to show signs of strain, as discussed below. Coupled with robust issue advertising—which does not explicitly call for election or defeat of candidates but typically praises or criticizes them in ways that could affect electoral outcomes—from interest groups, presidential candidates began looking toward the additional funding and lack of spending limits that private funds could provide. The emphasis on private funds continued into the 2000s, particularly after Barack Obama declined participating in any aspect of the public financing in 2008, and after the Supreme Court held in 2010 that corporations and unions could make unlimited independent expenditures calling for election or defeat of specific candidates. No major candidate accepted public funds in 2012, although three minor candidates participated.[64] Even supporters of the program generally concede that it is in need of significant reform to be attractive to contemporary candidates and to equip those candidates with sufficient resources to compete in the modern campaign environment. The following discussion explains the transition from public to private financing since the 1970s.

The Public Financing Program[65]

Congress created the presidential public financing program in the 1971 Revenue Act, which permitted individual taxpayers (except nonresident aliens) to designate $1 ($2 for married couples filing jointly) to the Presidential Election Campaign Fund (PECF), the account that houses public

---

[63] Although third-party candidates may qualify for public funds, they rarely do.

[64] These include Green Party nominee Jill Stein, Libertarian Party nominee and former Gov. Gary Johnson, and former Gov. Buddy Roemer (R). As noted elsewhere in this report, party affiliation for Johnson and Roemer vary depending on source and date consulted. As of this writing, the most recent FEC certification for public funds occurred in August 2012. At that time, total certifications were approximately $700,000. For additional discussion, see Federal Election Commission, "Federal Election Commission Certifies Federal Matching Funds for Jill Stein for President," press release, August 28, 2012, http://www.fec.gov/press/press2012/20120828_SteinMatchFund.shtml.

[65] For additional discussion of the public financing program, see CRS Report RL34534, *Public Financing of Presidential Campaigns: Overview and Analysis*, by R. Sam Garrett; CRS Report RL34630, *Federal Funding of Presidential Nominating Conventions: Overview and Policy Options*, by R. Sam Garrett and Shawn Reese; and CRS Report R41604, *Proposals to Eliminate Public Financing of Presidential Campaigns*, by R. Sam Garrett.

funds.[66] (The checkoff amounts were raised to $3 and $6 respectively in 1993.[67]) As noted previously, candidates first received public funds during the 1976 election cycle. Amounts in the PECF are diverted from the Treasury's general fund for use by qualified presidential candidates and party nominating conventions. Checkoff designations are the only revenue source for the public financing program, even if the Treasury Secretary projects that the fund will become insolvent.[68] Under current law, Congress makes no appropriation to the PECF.

The presidential public financing program provides funds for three phases of the campaign: (1) grants to nominating conventions; (2) matching funds for qualified primary candidates; and (3) grants for general-election nominees. Convention funding goes to the Democratic and Republican parties' (or qualifying third parties') convention committees; funding for the primary and general elections goes directly to qualifying candidates' campaigns.[69] Under federal law, convention funding receives priority, followed by general election grants and primary matching funds.[70] In other words, primary matching funds are distributed only if sufficient amounts remain after first providing convention grants and general-election grants. Prorated amounts may be distributed in the event of shortfalls (insufficient balances in the fund). Shortfalls have been of increasing concern in recent election cycles, although the fund has enjoyed surpluses since 2008 because of candidates choosing not to participate..[71]

How the Program Works

Public financing benefits are set by statute and vary by type of candidate and phase of the campaign.[72]

- For their *nominating conventions*, each of the two major parties may qualify for grants of $4 million as adjusted for inflation (approximately $16.8 million each in 2008).[73] For the 2012 election cycle, the Democratic and Republican convention committees each received grants of approximately $18.2 million.

---

[66] On the presidential public financing portion of the Revenue Act, see 85 Stat. 573. The checkoff essentially routes the designated portion of one's taxes paid to the PECF rather than to the general treasury. It does not affect one's tax refund or liability.

[67] 26 U.S.C. §6096(a). On the increase, see P.L. 103-66; 107 Stat. 567-568.

[68] See, for example, 26 U.S.C. §9006(c).

[69] For additional discussion of convention funding, see CRS Report RL34630, *Federal Funding of Presidential Nominating Conventions: Overview and Policy Options*, by R. Sam Garrett and Shawn Reese.

[70] On prioritization of convention funding, see 26 U.S.C. §9008(a).

[71] Prorated funds are distributed under the so-called "shortfall rule," which requires the Treasury Secretary to "seek to achieve an equitable distribution" among competing members of the same political party. See 26 U.S.C. §9037(b). Therefore, in the event of a shortfall, those competing for matching funds receive approximately the same amounts. IRS regulations permit payments as soon as funds become available (rather than on the monthly basis specified in Title 26 of the U.S. Code) in the event of a shortfall. See Department of the Treasury, Internal Revenue Service, "Payments From the Presidential Primary Matching Payment Account," 73 *Federal Register* 8608, February 14, 2008; and Department of the Treasury, Internal Revenue Service, "Payments From the Presidential Primary Matching Payment Account," 73 *Federal Register* 67103, November 13, 2008.

[72] Congress established the public financing program via the 1971 Revenue Act (for the relevant portion, see 85 Stat. 73). Amounts available to candidates appear in Title 26 of the U.S. Code (the Internal Revenue Code), as cited below. Separately, the following text does not cover lesser amounts available to third parties. As noted previously, third parties and their candidates rarely receive public funds. For additional discussion, see CRS Report RL34534, *Public Financing of Presidential Campaigns: Overview and Analysis*, by R. Sam Garrett.

[73] Ibid., 26 U.S.C. §9008(b); 26 U.S.C. §9008(b)(2). On application procedures, see 11 C.F.R. 9008.3. The 2008 figures (continued...)

- For the *general election*, the Democratic and Republican presidential nominees are eligible for $20 million grants, as adjusted for inflation (approximately $84.1 million each in 2008).[74] Third parties may qualify for lesser amounts. The FEC estimated that the general election grant would have been approximately $91.2 million for 2012 had any candidate participated.[75]

- When candidates most recently participated actively in public financing, in 2008 *primary* candidates could spend up to $42 million (plus approximately $14 million in fundraising, legal, and accounting costs, which are exempt from the base spending limit), but the amount of funds participants receive depends on their ability to secure government matching payments based on private fundraising. In 2012, the spending limit for publicly funded primary candidates was $45.6 million, although no candidate neared that amount. Participating candidates' individual contributions of up to $250 may be matched at a rate of 100% each. For example, a privately raised contribution of $200 would be matched for $200, bringing the candidate's total receipt of funds to $400. On the other hand, contributions of more than $250 are matched only for the first $250.[76] For example, a contribution of $1,000 would only be eligible for $250 in matching funds.[77] The primary matching fund program, which was designed to magnify small donations, applies only to individual contributions. PAC or party contributions are ineligible for matching payments. As noted above, the FEC certified approximately $700,000 in matching funds for minor candidates.[78]

Conditions on Participation

Publicly funded *primary* candidates must adhere to overall and state-specific spending limits.

(...continued)

were aggregated by the author from $16,356,000 in Federal Election Commission, "FEC Approves Matching Funds for 2008 Candidates," press release, at http://www.fec.gov/press/press2007/20071207cert.shtml and $464,760 in an inflation-adjustment figure provided by Wanda Thomas, deputy assistant staff director for public financing, FEC (e-mail correspondence with author, April 9, 2008). Conventions also receive additional federal funding for security. On that topic, see CRS Report RL34630, *Federal Funding of Presidential Nominating Conventions: Overview and Policy Options*, by R. Sam Garrett and Shawn Reese. Although the FEC certified the 2008 Republican National Convention for the full $16.8 million allocation, the committee ultimately received $13.0 million. The convention ended early due to Hurricane Gustav.

[74] 2 U.S.C. §§441a(b)(1); 441a(c). The 2008 amount appears in Federal Election Commission, "FEC Approves Matching Funds for 2008 Candidates."

[75] Federal Election Commission, "Roemer First Presidential Candidate Declared Eligible for Primary Matching Funds in 2012 Race," press release, February 3, 2012, http://www.fec.gov/press/press2012/20120202Roemer_MatchingFunds.shtml.

[76] The $250 cap applies to any single contribution or to small contributions from the same individual that aggregate more than $250. For example, a series of six $50 contributions (aggregating $300) would only be matched at $250.

[77] The base amount, without the inflation adjustment, is $10 million. On primary spending limits, see 2 U.S.C. §§441a(b)(1); 441a(c).

[78] This information appears in the February 29, 2012, U.S. Treasury Financial Management Service's (FMS) report on the financial status of the PECF, provided to CRS by FMS.

- All publicly financed campaigns must: agree to various record-keeping requirements, submit to FEC audits, and limit spending from the candidate's personal funds to no more than $50,000.[79]

- The aggregate limit was approximately $42 million in 2008 (plus approximately $14 million in fundraising, legal, and accounting costs, which are exempt from the base spending limit). State-specific limits in 2008 ranged from $841,000 in sparsely populated states and territories, to approximately $18.3 million in California. These amounts were (and are) determined by a formula established in FECA (the greater of 16¢ multiplied by the voting-age population (VAP) of the state, or $200,000, as adjusted for inflation).[80]

Publicly financed candidates in the *general* election must agree not to raise private funds for their campaigns. In exchange for the taxpayer-funded grant, their spending was limited to approximately $91.2 million in 2012.[81]

Declining Participation Over Time

Perhaps the most significant change in the campaign finance environment for recent presidential campaigns is the decline of the public financing program. This is true both for taxpayer designations through the checkoff and for candidate participation in the program. As **Figure 3** shows, checkoff participation reached a high point in 1980, when 28.7% of filers designated funds for the PECF. With minor exceptions, participation has fallen steadily since that time. Fewer than 15% of taxpayers have made public financing designations every calendar year since 1993. Taxpayer participation reached a low of 7.3% in 2009.[82] Despite a slight increase in 2010, for rounding purposes, the figure remained at 7.3%.[83]

---

[79] 26 U.S.C. §§9003(a); 9033(a). On the $50,000 limit, see 26 U.S.C. §9006(d).

[80] The base limit (before the inflation adjustment) is $10 million. See 2 U.S.C. §441a(b)1(A). For the 2008 limits, see Federal Election Commission, "Presidential Spending Limits for 2008," at http://www.fec.gov/pages/brochures/pubfund_limits_2008.shtml.

[81] The base limit (before the inflation adjustment) is $20 million. See 2 U.S.C. §441a(b)1(B).

[82] Checkoff percentage data since 2007 appear to be reported by fiscal year, whereas the pre-2007 data appear to be reported by calendar year.

[83] Financial Management Service data obtained via the FEC indicate that the 2009 rate was 7.27%, compared with 7.28% for 2010.

Figure 3. Taxpayer Participation in Public Financing Since 1976

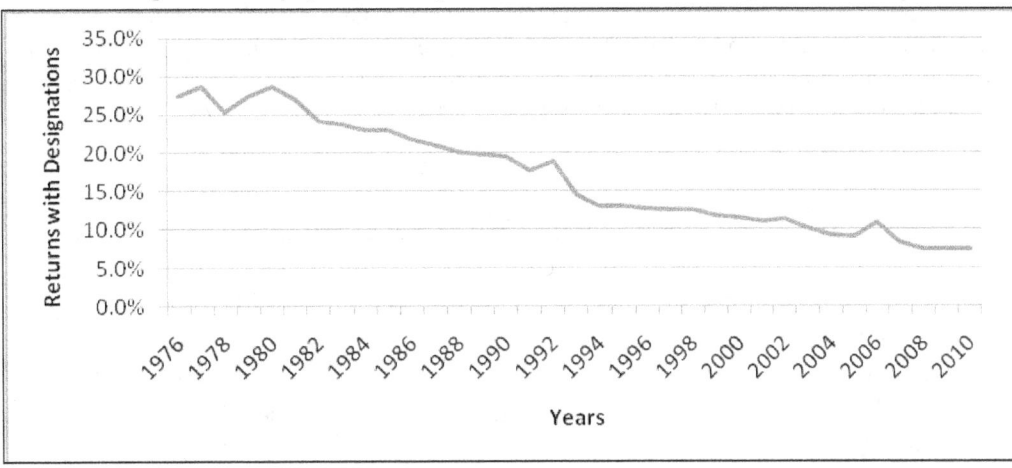

Source: CRS graph based on IRS data cited in Federal Election Commission, "Presidential Matching Fund Income Tax Check-Off Status," brochure, June 2008. FY2008-FY2010 data were provided separately to CRS by the FEC.

Although taxpayers have never heavily participated in public financing, every major presidential candidate since 1976 participated in at least the general-election phase of the program until 2008. Indeed, only a few wealthy, self-financed candidates declined to participate in public financing.[84] Beginning during the 2000 election cycle, however, some major candidates began to opt out of primary matching funds, apparently believing that bypassing required spending limits would be strategically advantageous. That year, George W. Bush participated in public financing during the general election but not during the primary. Then-candidate Bush was the first person elected President without having accepted both primary and general election public financing. In 2004, President Bush and Democratic nominee Senator John Kerry both declined public financing during the primary campaign.[85] Both accepted public funds for the general-election campaign.

Disparate Resources: Public versus Private Funds in 2008 and Beyond

The crowded field of competitive candidates and front-loaded primary calendar in 2008 contributed to fundraising pressures early in the cycle.[86] As shown in **Table 5**, eight candidates received primary matching funds in 2008. The Democratic and Republican parties also both received funding for their nominating conventions.[87] In the general election in 2008, Republican nominee John McCain accepted the $84.1 million public financing grant. Democratic nominee Barack Obama became the first person elected President without having participated in any

---

[84] Examples include Ross Perot (1992) and Steve Forbes (1996).

[85] Federal Election Commission, "FEC Approves Matching Funds for 2004 Presidential Candidates," final certifications, press release, April 1, 2005, at http://www.fec.gov/press/press2005/20050401cert.html. See also Anthony Corrado, "Public Funding of Presidential Campaigns," p. 184.

[86] Anthony Corrado, "Fund-raising Strategies in the 2008 Presidential Campaign," in *Campaigns and Elections American Style*, ed. James A. Thurber and Candice J. Nelson, 3rd ed. (Boulder, CO: Westview, 2010), pp. 105-136.

[87] See Federal Election Commission, "FEC Approves Matching Funds for 2008 Candidates," press release, December 20, 2007, at http://www.fec.gov/press/press2007/20071207cert.shtml for a base certification of $16,356,000. The FEC also certified an additional payment, to cover inflation, of $464,760. Information on the inflation adjustment comes from e-mail correspondence between the author and Wanda Thomas, deputy assistant staff director for public financing, FEC, April 9, 2008. The convention refunded the remaining amount of the 2008 allocation.

aspect of the public financing program. Accepting public funding in the general election relieved the McCain campaign of private fundraising obligations (although publicly funded candidates nonetheless may continue to raise private funds for limited legal and accounting expenses and joint fundraising ventures with party committees). It also meant that the campaign could spend no more in the general election than the $84.1 million it received in public funds.

Table 5. Public Financing to 2008 Presidential Candidates

Candidate	Campaign	Amount
Joseph Biden	Primary	$2.0 million
Christopher Dodd	Primary	$2.0 million
John Edwards	Primary	$12.9 million
Mike Gravel	Primary	$0.2 million
Duncan Hunter	Primary	$0.5 million
Dennis Kucinich	Primary	$1.1 million
John McCain	General	$84.1 million
Ralph Nader	Primary	$0.9 million
Thomas Tancredo	Primary	$2.3 million
Total	**Primary and General**	**$106.0 million**

Source: CRS analysis of FEC certifications and Treasury Department, Financial Management Service, payment data.

Notes: Amounts for individual candidates are rounded to the nearest hundred-thousand dollars. The total is rounded to the nearest million dollars. The table does not include funds initially certified for Senator McCain's campaign, which applied for primary matching funds but later withdrew from public financing during the primary campaign.

The Obama campaign, meanwhile, could raise and spend unlimited amounts because it opted out of public financing.[88] The $747.8 million the Obama campaign raised—partially by tapping a vast network of contributors who gave less than $200 and through successful online fundraising—far exceeded previous records.[89] Indeed, even with accepting unlimited private funds in the primary election, the McCain campaign raised less than half ($351.5 million) as much as the Obama campaign, as shown in **Figure 4**. The Obama campaign's fundraising prowess also far outpaced the privately financed Hillary Clinton campaign ($223.9 million) in the long Democratic primary.

---

[88] Of course, contributions must be solicited and raised within the limits established in FECA. Overall, however, there is no aggregate fundraising or spending limit for privately financed candidates.

[89] The $747.8 million figure comes from CRS analysis of FEC data cited throughout this section. On Obama campaign small donor activity, see, for example, Anthony Corrado, "Fund-raising Strategies in the 2008 Presidential Campaign," in *Campaigns and Elections American Style*, ed. James A. Thurber and Candice J. Nelson, 3rd ed. (Boulder, CO: Westview, 2010), pp. 114-120; Campaign Finance Institute, "All CFI Funding Statistics Revised And Updated For The 2008 Presidential Primary And General Election Candidates," press release, January 8, 2010, http://www.cfinst.org/Press/PReleases/10-01-08/Revised_and_Updated_2008_Presidential_Statistics.aspx.; and Michael Malbin, "Small Donors, Large Donors, and the Internet: Rethinking Public Financing After Obama," in *Public Financing in American Elections*, ed. Costas Panagopoulos (Philadelphia: Temple University Press, 2011), pp. 36-61.

Figure 4. Total Fundraising by Selected 2008 Presidential Campaigns

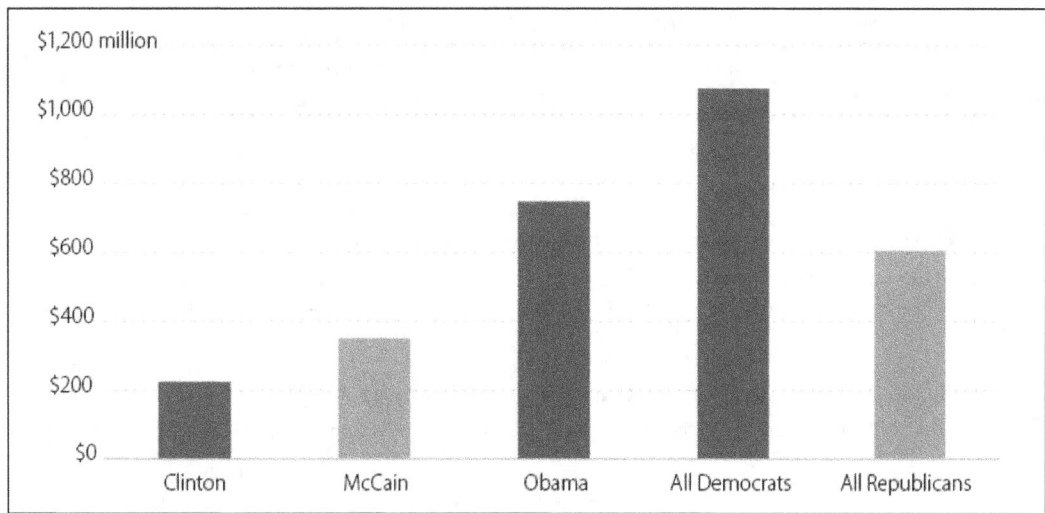

Source: CRS analysis of FEC data, http://www.fec.gov/disclosurep/pnational.do.

These developments, combined with declining PECF balances due to low levels of taxpayer participation (discussed above), have placed the public financing program's future viability in doubt. Even those who support the program have proposed significant reforms to make public financing more attractive to candidates. Legislation to that effect has been regularly introduced in recent Congresses, as have bills to eliminate the program.[90]

As **Table 6** and **Table 7** show (see also **Figure 5**), as of August 2012 (the latest data available as of this writing), Democratic and Republican presidential candidates had raised approximately $855.8 million for the 2012 election cycle. Democratic fundraising of $432.2.million accounted for a slight majority of that amount (approximately 50.5%). The figures do not reflect other fundraising that might also benefit presidential campaigns, such as by the national party committees.

---

[90] See CRS Report RL34534, *Public Financing of Presidential Campaigns: Overview and Analysis*, by R. Sam Garrett; CRS Report RL34630, *Federal Funding of Presidential Nominating Conventions: Overview and Policy Options*, by R. Sam Garrett and Shawn Reese; and CRS Report R41604, *Proposals to Eliminate Public Financing of Presidential Campaigns*, by R. Sam Garrett.

Table 6. 2012 Presidential Campaign Contributions Received by Party

Data are current through August 31, 2012 (reported September 20, 2012)

Candidate	Contributions
All Democrats	$432.2 million
All Republicans	421.1 million
All Candidates	$855.8 million

Source: Federal Election Commission data, http://www.fec.gov/disclosurep/pnational.do.

Notes: The table excludes candidates who are not generally recognized as national political figures. Third-party and independent candidates are also excluded. Numbers in the table and in the underlying data used to populate the table are rounded and therefore do not sum in all cases.

Table 7. 2012 Presidential Campaign Receipts by Candidate and Party

Data are current through August 31, 2012 (reported September 20, 2012)

Party	Candidate	Contributions
Republican	Michelle Bachmann	$10.3 million
Republican	Herman Cain	$16.3 million
Republican	Jon Huntsman	$8.8 million
Republican	Newt Gingrich	$23.3 million
Republican*	Gary Johnson	$1.8 million
Republican	Thaddeus McCotter	$0.5 million
Democrat	Barack Obama	$432.2 million
Republican	Tim Pawlenty	$5.2 million
Republican	Ron Paul	$40.7 million
Republican	Rick Perry	$19.7 million
Republican*	Buddy Roemer	$0.7 million
Republican	Mitt Romney	$274.0 million
Republican	Rick Santorum	$22.3 million

Source: CRS analysis of Federal Election Commission data, http://www.fec.gov/disclosurep/pnational.do.

Notes: The table excludes candidates who are not generally recognized as national political figures. Third-party and independent candidates are also excluded. Party affiliations are the same as those listed in the FEC source data. Numbers in the table are rounded. *Party affiliation for candidates Johnson and Roemer has varied in FEC data throughout the election cycle, likely because of differing party status listed in different states. For ease of presentation, both candidates are listed here as Republicans, but may appear elsewhere under "Libertarian" or "Other" labels.

Figure 5. 2012 Presidential Campaign Receipts by Candidate and Party

Data are current through August 31, 2012 (reported September 20, 2012)

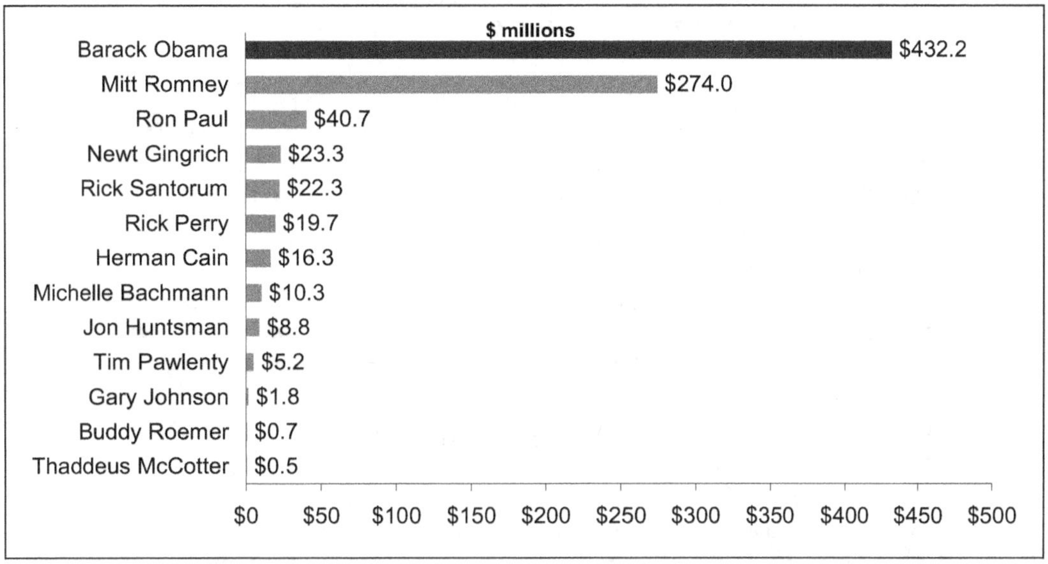

Source: CRS analysis of Federal Election Commission data, http://www.fec.gov/disclosurep/pnational.do.

Notes: The figure excludes candidates who are not generally recognized as national political figures. Third-party and independent candidates are also excluded. Numbers in the figure are rounded. *Party affiliation for candidates Johnson and Roemer has varied in FEC data throughout the election cycle, likely because of differing party status listed in different states. For ease of presentation, both candidates are listed here as Republicans, but may appear elsewhere under "Libertarian" or "Other" labels.

Outside Money: Spending by Parties, PACs, and Other Groups

In addition to amounts raised and spent by the campaigns themselves, noncandidate organizations can also play a key role in presidential campaigns. These funds, often characterized as "outside" money for their separation from candidate campaigns, have been especially prominent in recent election cycles. The types of funds, groups, and which laws and regulations apply to the groups can vary substantially with individual circumstances. In the broadest sense, noncandidate activity can be divided into fundraising and spending by entities known as "political committees" and "non-political committees."

Political committees (which also include candidate committees) are party committees and PACs. Political committees are primarily regulated by FECA and the FEC. Non-political committees most prominently include entities known as "political organizations," as regulated under the Internal Revenue Code (IRC) administered by the Internal Revenue Service (IRS). In particular, they include groups regulated as Section 501(c)(4) social welfare organizations, 501(c)(5) labor unions, and 501(c)(6) trade associations. They also include Section 527 organizations—groups whose activities might influence elections but which are not considered political committees.[91]

The degree to which an entity can coordinate its activities with a political campaign is limited—and in some cases, prohibited.[92] Although the details of coordination are beyond the scope of this report, the important point for the general discussion here is that outside organizations are limited in the ways in which they can support candidate campaigns, as briefly summarized below.[93]

- Political parties and PACs (but not super PACs, discussed below) can contribute directly to presidential campaigns, up to the amounts specified in FECA and shown in **Table 4**.[94]

- Party committees may make coordinated expenditures, subject to limits, supporting their presidential candidates. In 2008, the Democratic and Republican parties were limited to $19.2 million in coordinated expenditures supporting their presidential candidates. The 2012 limit is approximately $21.7 million.

- In the aftermath of *Citizens United*, as discussed previously, corporations and unions (including incorporated entities such as 501(c)(4) social welfare organizations) may make IEs explicitly calling for election or defeat of a federal candidate. Parties and PACs may also make IEs, as they could before *Citizens United*. Super PACs also provide an option for IEs supporting or opposing presidential candidates.

- Non-political committees may make electioneering communications (ECs) that refer to clearly identified federal candidates during pre-election periods but do not explicitly call for their election or defeat. These communications are also sometimes known as "issue advertisements," signifying their focus on policy issues rather than electoral issues.[95] Congress originally established the EC

[91] As the term is commonly used, "527" refers to groups registered with the Internal Revenue Service (IRS) as section 527 political organizations that seemingly intend to influence federal elections in ways that place them outside the FECA definition of a political committee. By contrast, political committees (which include candidate committees, party committees, and political action committees) are regulated by the FEC and federal election law. There is a debate regarding which 527s are required to register with the FEC as political committees. FEC contributor disclosure for these organizations applies only to those who designate their contributions for use in independent expenditures or electioneering communications. For additional discussion, see CRS Report RS22895, *527 Groups and Campaign Activity: Analysis Under Campaign Finance and Tax Laws*, by L. Paige Whitaker and Erika K. Lunder.

[92] Coordination is a complex topic that is beyond the scope of this report. In brief, limits on coordination between campaigns and other political committees or outside organizations are intended to prevent circumvention of contribution limits. On coordination and the three-part regulatory test for coordination, see, respectively 2 U.S.C. §441a(a)(7)(B) and 11 C.F.R. §109.21. For additional discussion, see CRS Report RS22644, *Coordinated Party Expenditures in Federal Elections: An Overview*, by R. Sam Garrett and L. Paige Whitaker.

[93] Although not discussed here, party committees have also pursued hybrid advertising and joint fundraising committees, which benefit multiple candidates. For additional discussion, see CRS Report R40091, *Campaign Finance: Potential Legislative and Policy Issues for the 111th Congress*, by R. Sam Garrett.

[94] In the case of a contribution to a publicly financed presidential candidate in the primary, contributions from parties or PACs would not be eligible for PECF matching funds. In the general election, publicly financed candidates are prohibited from accepting private contributions.

[95] The terms "issue advertisements" or "issue advertising" are not exclusive to ECs, which, by definition, must meet certain timing requirements and other criteria. For additional discussion, see, for example, CRS Report R41542, *The State of Campaign Finance Policy: Recent Developments and Issues for Congress*, by R. Sam Garrett; and CRS Report RL30669, *The Constitutionality of Campaign Finance Regulation: Buckley v. Valeo and Its Supreme Court Progeny*, by L. Paige Whitaker. See also 2 U.S.C. §434(f)(3).

concept in BCRA to target "sham" issue ads that urged voters to form opinions about candidates in ways that many observers believed influenced electoral outcomes. In the wake of *Citizens United*, it is unclear how prominent ECs will continue to be, as corporations and unions may now engage in IEs that directly advocate for or against candidates.

Of these categories of "outside" spending, IEs and ECs are perhaps the most notable because, unlike contributions and coordinated party expenditures, IEs and ECs cannot be constitutionally limited.[96] In addition, unlike generic issue advertising that does not refer to federal candidates, IEs and ECs clearly refer to particular presidential candidates. As **Figure 6** shows, particularly since 2004, both types of spending have been prominent in presidential elections. Specifically, IEs and ECs accounted for $445.9 million between 1996 and 2008. Of that amount, virtually all ($429.8 million) was spent in 2004 and 2008. As the figure shows, like much political advertising, IEs more typically oppose candidates than support candidates.[97]

Figure 6. Selected Outside Spending in Presidential Campaigns, 1996-2008

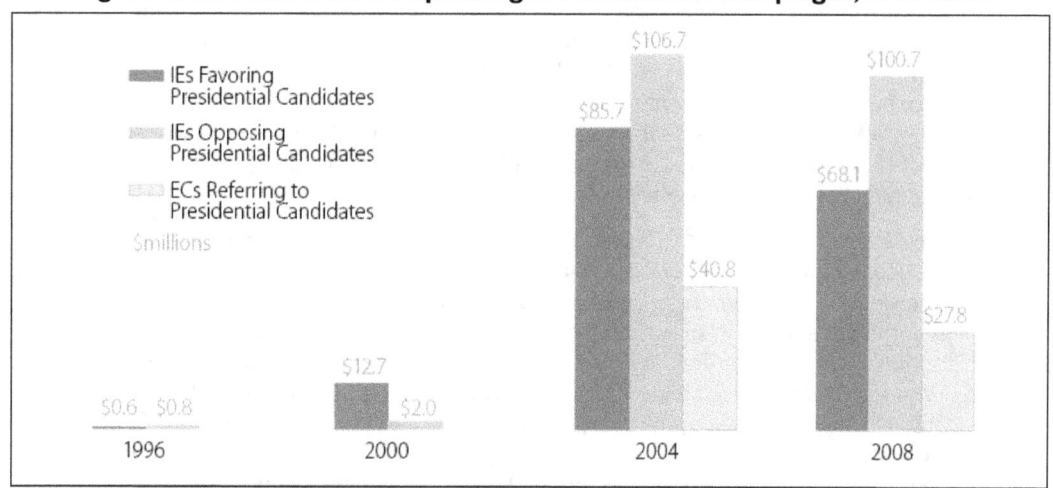

Source: CRS analysis of FEC "Overview of Presidential Financial Activity 1996 – 2008" file, http://www.fec.gov/press/press2009/20090608PresStat.shtml.

---

[96] Unlimited campaign spending, except as a condition of participation in public financing, was established in *Buckley*. For additional discussion, see CRS Report RL30669, *The Constitutionality of Campaign Finance Regulation: Buckley v. Valeo and Its Supreme Court Progeny*, by L. Paige Whitaker.

[97] Whether or not political advertising that opposes candidates is "negative" is subject to substantial debate. See, for example, Michael M. Franz et al., *Campaign Advertising and American Democracy* (Philadelphia: Temple University Press, 2008); John G. Geer, *In Defense of Negativity: Attack Ads in Presidential Campaigns* (Chicago: University of Chicago Press, 2006); and *Crowded Airwaves: Campaign Advertising in Elections*, ed. James A. Thurber, Candice J. Nelson, and David A. Dulio (Washington: Brookings Institution Press, 2000). EC reports do not include support or opposition information, as these expenditures do not include express advocacy messages.

Notes: Electioneering communication reports were first filed during the 2004 election cycle. The increase between 2000 and 2004 is likely due to increased IE reporting by 527 organizations, shifting party strategies away from soft money post-BCRA, and the particularly competitive nature of the election. Numbers in the figure are rounded.

The Outlook for 2012

Because *Citizens United*, *SpeechNow*, and related developments were not in effect during the 2008 election cycle, the scope of outside spending in 2012 may be even greater than discussed above. Just a few selected examples of fundraising and spending developments in 2012 demonstrate that candidates and their allies and opponents raised and spent tremendous sums to capture the presidency:[98]

- By September 30, 2011, major presidential candidates had reported raising more than $175 million. Less than one year later, in August 2012, that figure had increased almost five fold to approximately $855 million.

- By September 30, 2011, the Obama for America committee—President Obama's principal campaign committee and reelection campaign organization—reported raising $86.2 million for the 2012 cycle. That amount is $2 million more than the entire public financing allocation for a general-election nominee in 2008 ($84.1 million). Given the pace of subsequent fundraising among Democratic and Republican candidates and the presence of heavy outside spending, no major-party nominee accepted public funds in 2012.

- In the aftermath of *Citizens United*, *SpeechNow*, and FEC activity, super PACs have pledged to raise millions of dollars to influence the 2012 elections. These groups provide another outlet for individual contributors, as well as the potential for corporate and union spending. Nonconnected PACs that choose to do so may also raise and spend unlimited amounts for independent expenditures per the *Carey* scenario discussed above. CRS discusses both topics elsewhere.[99] Although super PACs are prohibited from coordinating their activities with candidate campaigns, some of the most prominent super PACs operating in 2012 appear to have close ties with, or employ directly, staff members who have close personal or professional ties with presidential candidates. Whether these relationships circumvent the spirit of limits on campaign coordination is a contentious point of debate.[100]

- In some cases, spending among super PACs that appear to be devoted primarily to electing a particular presidential candidate is rivaling or outpacing the financial activity of the candidates themselves. For example, in January 2012, when heavy fundraising and spending occurred before and during key primaries and caucuses, pro-Mitt Romney super PAC Restore Our Future and the Romney

---

[98] Unless otherwise noted, information in this section comes from CRS analysis of various FEC data.

[99] See CRS Report R42042, *Super PACs in Federal Elections: Overview and Issues for Congress*, by R. Sam Garrett; and CRS Report R41542, *The State of Campaign Finance Policy: Recent Developments and Issues for Congress*, by R. Sam Garrett.

[100] For additional discussion of these and related points regarding 2012 presidential activity, see, for example, Kenneth P. Doyle, "New PAC Ads Feature Gov. Perry as FEC Considers Ruling on Coordination Issues," *Daily Report for Executives*, November 9, 2011, p. A-10, DER 217; and "The Campaign Jungle," *New York Times*, November 13, 2011, p. SR-10, New York edition.

for President campaign both reported raising approximately $6.6 million. Also in January, Winning Our Future, a super PAC that promotes Newt Gingrich's presidential candidacy, reported spending $9.9 million—$4 million more (68%) than the $5.9 million spent by the candidate's campaign. On the Democratic side, however, the Obama reelection campaign's financial activity has outpaced super PACs. For example, for February 2012, super PAC Priorities USA Action reported having raised $2 million, compared with $21.3 million for the Obama reelection campaign.[101]

- Transparency among IE donors has been a concern in recent years, but may particularly be so in 2012 given post-*Citizens United* avenues for political donations (especially super PACs). Despite disclosure requirements, the original source of some contributions that ultimately support IEs are not reported to the FEC if the source did not specify that the donation was intended to further IEs.[102]

Thus far, this report has discussed the major contemporary issues surrounding how candidates secure their party's nomination for the presidency and how campaign finance law and practice facilitate and constrain key elements of the campaign. Candidates, voters, political parties, and various interest groups are central players in the campaign for the primary nomination and in the general election. The electoral college phase of the election is separate from the campaign season and the popular vote, but its role in choosing a President and Vice President is rooted in the Constitution and political tradition. The report now turns to this essential final step in presidential selection.

The Electoral College System: Contemporary Trends[103]

One of the many compromises incorporated into the U.S. Constitution, the electoral college represented an effort by the Philadelphia Convention of 1787 to provide for a presidential election that would

- be free of undue influence by Congress, thus insuring greater independence in the executive;

- provide a fundamental role for the states by establishing the election as a federal, rather than national, process;

- allocate electors by a formula that provided some advantage to less populous states;

---

[101] This information comes from CRS analysis of January 2012 political committee reports filed with the FEC in February 2012.

[102] For example, if a corporation made an unrestricted contribution to a trade association, which in turn contributed those funds to a super PAC that used them for an IE, the trade association—not the corporation—would be reported as the IE donor. For additional discussion of disclosure requirements, see CRS Report R42042, *Super PACs in Federal Elections: Overview and Issues for Congress*, by R. Sam Garrett and CRS Report R41542, *The State of Campaign Finance Policy: Recent Developments and Issues for Congress*, by R. Sam Garrett.

[103] Thomas H. Neale (x7-7883), Specialist in American National Government, authored this section.

- give the states wide-ranging authority over the means by which they would choose their electors: democratically, by popular vote, by the legislature itself, or by another body altogether; and, ultimately;

- temper popular enthusiasms and partisan and sectional attachments by giving the actual vote to the electors, who, it was hoped, would be prominent citizens of their states and communities, well-informed and educated persons who would make a balanced and measured selection.

Whatever the founders' intentions, from the very beginning, the electoral college began to change almost immediately, through constitutional amendment, state laws, and political party practices. The growth of political parties and the spread of voting rights and democratic principles overtook the founders' vision within two decades, and the electoral college system evolved into the compound system that continues to govern U.S presidential elections two centuries later.

The Electoral College System Today

The United States is almost unique among contemporary democratic republics in that its President and Vice President are elected indirectly, on a federal basis, rather than directly by popular vote on a nationwide basis. The fundamentals of the electoral college system were established by Article II, Section 1 of the U.S. Constitution, and subsequently revised by the 12th Amendment. The Constitution's minimal provisions have been complemented over the past two centuries by a range of federal and state laws, political party procedures, and enduring political traditions, leading to the system as it exists today. The salient features of the contemporary system, a mixture of these elements, are detailed below.

Components of the Electoral College

The electors are collectively known as the electoral college; although this phrase does not appear in the Constitution, it gained currency in the early days of the republic, and was recognized in federal law in 1845.[104] The electoral college has no continuing existence; its sole purpose is to elect the President and Vice President. Each state is allocated a number of electors equal to the combined total of its U.S. Senate and House of Representatives delegations.[105] The District of Columbia is also allocated three electors.[106] At present, the total is 538, reflecting the combined size of the Senate (100 Members), the House (435 Members), and the District of Columbia electors. Any person may serve as an elector, except Senators and Representatives, or any other person holding an office of "trust or profit" under the United States.[107] The legislatures of the several states select the method by which electors are chosen.[108] In practice, all states currently provide for popular election of their electoral college delegations.[109] Candidates for the office of elector are nominated by political parties and other groups eligible to be on the ballot in each

---

[104] 3 U.S.C. §4.

[105] U.S. Constitution, Article II, Section 1.

[106] Ibid., 23rd Amendment.

[107] Ibid., Article II, Section 1.

[108] Ibid.

[109] Neal Peirce and Lawrence Longley, *The People's President, The Electoral College in American History and the Direct Vote Alternative*, rev. ed. (New Haven: Yale University Press, 1981), pp. 44-47.

state. In most cases, the elector candidates are nominated by the state party committee or the party's statewide convention.[110] The winning candidates must gain a majority of electoral votes, currently 270 of 538, in order to be elected. If no ticket of candidates attains a majority, then the House of Representatives elects the President, and the Senate the Vice President, in a procedure known as contingent election.[111]

How The Electoral College Functions

Presidential Election Day is set by law for Tuesday after the first Monday in November every fourth year succeeding the election of President and Vice President.[112] Presidential Election Day falls on November 6 in 2012. On Presidential Election Day, voters across the country cast *one* vote for the team of candidates for President and Vice President they support. When they do so, however, they are actually voting for the political party "ticket" of electors supporting, and pledged to vote for, that party's team of presidential and vice presidential candidates.[113] Popular votes are cast, electors are chosen, and electoral votes are cast on a state-by-state basis. While the nationwide vote count is given considerable publicity, it is the vote in the states that decides the election.

The goal of presidential campaigns is to win by carrying states that collectively cast a majority of electoral votes. In particular, political parties and individual presidential campaigns give attention to states that are closely contested, or that have large delegations of electoral votes, or both. Winning a majority of the more populous "battleground" states is considered crucial to obtaining the necessary electoral vote majority.

In 48 states and the District of Columbia, the presidential/vice presidential ticket winning the most popular votes (a plurality or more) in that state is awarded all of its electoral votes. That is to say, the winning party's entire ticket of electors is elected. This is referred to as the "winner-take-all" or "general ticket" system. Maine and Nebraska use a different method of allocating electoral votes, the "district" system. Under this method, popular votes are counted twice, first, on a statewide basis, and second, on a congressional district basis. The presidential/vice presidential ticket receiving the most votes statewide receives two electors/electoral votes for this total. The ticket winning the most votes in each congressional district receives a single elector/electoral vote for that district. In this way, a state's electoral vote may be divided to reflect geographical differences in support within the state for different candidates.[114]

Presidential electors assemble on the first Monday after the second Wednesday in December following the general election.[115] In 2012, the electors will assemble on December 17. They meet

---

[110] See U.S. Congress, Senate, *Nomination and Election of the President and Vice President of the United States, 2008*, "Part IV. State Laws Relating to the Nomination and Election of Presidential Electors." S. Doc. 111-15 (Washington: GPO, 2010), pp. 346-444.

[111] For more detailed information on the contingent election process, please consult CRS Report R40504, *Contingent Election of the President and Vice President by Congress: Perspectives and Contemporary Analysis*, by Thomas H. Neale.

[112] 3 U.S.C. §1.

[113] For individual state provisions, see *Nomination and Election of the President and Vice President*, pp. 310-345.

[114] For individual state requirements, see Ibid.

[115] 3 U.S.C. §7.

in their respective states, not collectively, and cast separate votes by ballot for the President and Vice President.[116]

As noted earlier, candidates for the office of elector are selected by their respective political party. They are expected to vote for the presidential and vice presidential candidates to whom they are pledged.[117] Some states seek to require them to so vote by law or other means, but most constitutional scholars hold that the electors remain free agents under the Constitution, and that they may vote for any person they choose.[118] On rare occasions, an elector will vote for a different candidate, or abstain from casting his or her vote for any candidate/s. They are known as "faithless electors."[119]

After the electoral college votes, the results are sent by state authorities to Congress and various other federal authorities designated by law. On January 6 of the year following a presidential election, Congress meets in a joint session to count the electoral votes and make a formal declaration of which candidates have been elected President and Vice President.[120]

Criticism and Defense of the Electoral College

The electoral college and the presidential election system that was built around it have been the subject of criticism since the earliest days of the Republic.

The primary contemporary criticism of the founders' creation is philosophical. Proponents of change maintain that the electoral college system is fundamentally undemocratic—it provides for "indirect" election of the President and Vice President. This, they assert, is an 18th century anachronism, dating from a time when communications were poor, the literacy rate was much lower, and the nation had yet to develop the durable, sophisticated, and inclusive democratic political system it now enjoys. They maintain that only direct popular election of the President and Vice President is consistent with modern democratic values and practice. Survey research consistently shows broad popular support for direct election. In its most recent question on the issue, the Gallup Poll reported that 62% of respondents favored an amendment providing for direct popular election, while 35% favored retention of the electoral college. This finding mirrors those recorded by Gallup as early as 1967.[121]

---

[116] U.S. Constitution, Article II, Section 1; 12th Amendment. The words "by ballot" are interpreted to mean by paper ballot. With respect to the location of meetings of the electors, the founders reasoned that if they met in their respective states, there would be less opportunity for political intrigue and chicanery than if they assembled in a single location. The difficulties inherent in long-distance travel at the time may also have influenced the Constitutional Convention's decision.

[117] For individual state requirements, see *Nomination and Election of the President and Vice President*, pp. 310-345.

[118] See *U.S. Constitution, Analysis and Interpretation, "The Constitution Annotated,"* Article II Analysis, Article II, Section 1, clauses 2-4, Election: Electors as Free Agents, available online to Members of Congress and staff at http://crs.gov/conan/default.aspx?mode=topic&doc=Article02.xml&t=1|4&s=1&c=2.

[119] For further information, see Project Fairvote, "Faithless Electors," available online at http://archive.fairvote.org/e_college/faithless.htm.

[120] 3 U.S.C. §15-18. The same sections of the U.S. Code provide for challenges to electoral votes, as occurred in 2001 and 2005.

[121] Lydia Saad, "Americans Would Swap Electoral College for Popular Vote," *The Gallup Poll*, October 24, 2011, available at http://www.gallup.com/poll/150245/americans-swap-electoral-college-popular-vote.aspx .

Beyond their fundamental challenge to the electoral college system, critics cite what they identify as a wide range of technical flaws. Perhaps the most prominent of these is that the electoral college system can lead to the election of Presidents who win the electoral vote, but gain fewer popular votes than their major opponent. This condition, often termed a "misfire," occurs primarily because of the nearly universal reliance on the "winner-take-all" or general ticket system in the states. Under these circumstances, a presidential ticket can gain an electoral college majority, but actually win fewer votes than its opponents. This happened in 1876, 1888, and, most recently, in 2000, when Democratic candidates Al Gore, Jr. and Joseph Lieberman gained 50,992,335 popular votes to 50,455,156 for Republican candidates George W. Bush and Richard Cheney.[122] The Republican nominees were elected, however, having won 30 states with 271 electoral votes, while their Democratic opponents took 20 states and the District of Columbia with 266 electoral votes.[123]

Other points of contention include the general ticket system itself, which is said to unfairly allocate electoral votes on a winner-take-all basis, rather than proportionally to reflect the vote in each state; the faithless elector phenomenon; the Constitution's provisions for contingent election by Congress in the event no candidate wins an electoral college majority;[124] the system's alleged "biases" in favor of populous states, less populous states and ethnic minorities; and the fact that electoral vote allocations do not reflect population change between reapportionments, the so-called decennial census bias.[125]

Defenders of the electoral college system reject the suggestion that it is undemocratic—electors are chosen by the voters in free elections. They note that the system prescribes a federal election of the President with votes tallied in each state. The United States is a federal republic, in which the states have a role in many areas of governance, including presidential elections. The Founders, they note, intended that choosing the President would be an action American voters take both as citizens of the United States, and as members of their state communities.

Further, defenders reject the suggestion that less populous states have an unfair advantage when compared to more populous states. Any modest mathematical advantage conveyed by the assignment of two electors to all states, regardless of size, is outmatched by the "voting power" advantage conferred on states such as California, whose 55 electoral votes constitute more than 20% of the number needed to win the presidency.[126] They also find the "faithless elector"

---

[122] *Congressional Quarterly's Guide to U.S. Elections*, 4th ed. (Washington: CQ Press, 2001), vol. 1, p. 688.

[123] One District of Columbia elector cast a blank ballot in protest against the outcome.

[125] For further information on these alleged technical biases, see Gordon J. Hylton, "How Much Difference Does the Small State Advantage in the Electoral College Really Make?" *Marquette University Faculty Law School Blog*, March 8, 2010, available online at http://law.marquette.edu/facultyblog/2010/03/08/how-much-difference-does-the-small-state-advantage-in-the-electoral-college-really-make/; Lawrence D. Longley and James D. Dana, Jr., "The Biases of the Electoral College in the 1990s," *Polity*, vol. 25, no. 1, autumn, 1992, pp. 123-45 (the author of this section has been unable to identify any studies updating Professor Longley's work since his death in 2002); and U.S. Federal Election Commission, National Clearinghouse on Election Administration, *The Electoral College*, by William C. Kimberling, Washington, 1992, p. 12. Representatives of the American Jewish Congress and the National Urban League also cited this advantage in Senate Subcommittee on the Constitution hearings in 1979. See U.S. Congress, Senate, Committee on the Judiciary, Subcommittee on the Constitution, *Direct Election of the President and Vice President of the United States*, hearings on S.J.Res. 28, 96th Congress, 1st session, March 27, 30, April 3, 9, 1979 (Washington: GPO, 1979), pp. 163-219.

[126] For additional information on the voting power theory, please consult CRS Report RL30804, *The Electoral College: An Overview and Analysis of Reform Proposals*, by L. Paige Whitaker and Thomas H. Neale.

---

argument to be specious.[127] Only nine such electoral votes have been cast against instructions since 1820, and none has ever influenced the outcome of an election. Nearly all electoral college reform plans would remove even this slim possibility for mischief by eliminating the office of elector.

Finally, they assert that the electoral college system promotes political stability. Parties and candidates must conduct ideologically broad-based campaigns throughout the nation in hopes of assembling a majority of electoral votes. The consequent need to forge national coalitions having a wide appeal has been a contributing factor in the moderation and stability of the nation and the two-party system.

Congressional Efforts to Reform the Electoral College by Constitutional Amendment, 1948-1979

From the late 1940s through 1979, a series of lively debates took place in Congress on the subject of electoral college reform. Throughout this period, hundreds of electoral college reform proposals were introduced in both chambers. They generally centered on one of two courses: "end it" by eliminating the entire electoral college system and establishing direct popular election, or "mend it" by reforming its more controversial provisions.[128] The question of electoral college reform or replacement was given active consideration by Congress throughout this period. Proposed amendments were the subject of hearings in the Senate and House Judiciary Committees on 17 different occasions between 1948 and 1979, and, most notably, electoral college reform proposals were debated in the full Senate on five occasions, and twice in the House during this period. Proposals were approved by the necessary two-thirds majority twice in the Senate and once in the House, but never in the same Congress.[129]

Following the 1979 defeat of a direct popular election amendment on the Senate floor, and the 1980 departure of Senator Birch Bayh, a prominent advocate for direct popular election, the question of electoral college reform largely disappeared from public attention and Congress's legislative agenda. Although Senators and Representatives continued to introduce reform proposals, few received any more action than routine committee referral, and in time, the number of measures introduced dropped almost to zero.[130] Even after the presidential election of 2000, which featured a so-called "misfire," there was little evidence of support in Congress for electoral

---

[127] Faithless electors are those who cast their votes for candidates other than those to whom they are pledged. Notwithstanding political party rules and state laws, most constitutional scholars believe that electors remain free agents, guided, but not bound, to vote for the candidates they were elected to support. For further information, see ibid.

[128] The three principal reform proposals would all eliminate the office of elector, and distribute electoral votes on the basis of different criteria. They were, and remain: (1) the automatic system, which would award electoral votes "automatically" in each state on a winner-take-all basis; (2) the district system, which would incorporate the system currently in place in Maine and Nebraska (see earlier in this report under "How the Electoral College Functions);" and (3) the proportional system, which would award votes in each state in direct proportion to the percentage of popular votes won by competing tickets in that state. For example, assume that a state is allocated 10 electoral votes, and that Ticket A received 60% of the state popular vote for President and Vice President, while Ticket B received 40%. Ticket A would be awarded six electoral votes, and Ticket B four.

[129] For a detailed examination and analysis of these efforts, see Peirce and Longley, *The People's President: The Electoral College in American History and the Direct Vote Alternative,* rev. ed. pp. 131-206.

[130] Only one relevant amendment, H.J.Res. 36, introduced by Rep. Jesse L. Jackson, Jr., which is discussed below, has been proposed to date in the 112th Congress. By comparison, 41 amendments related to direct election or electoral college reform were introduced in the 95th Congress (1977-1978).

---

college reform.[131] Moreover, the system performed very much in accord with contemporary expectations in the presidential election of 2008. Democratic candidates Barack Obama and Joseph Biden were able to translate a 7% popular vote margin of 52.9% (69,457,000) to 45.7% (59,935,000) for Republican contenders John McCain and Sarah Palin, into an overwhelming electoral vote of 365 votes (67.9%) to 173 (32.1%).[132]

Proposals to replace the electoral college system with direct popular election continue to be introduced in every Congress, albeit far fewer than in earlier years. For instance, H.J.Res. 36, introduced in the 112th Congress by Representative Jesse L. Jackson, Jr., and 29 co-sponsors, provides that "the President and Vice President shall be elected jointly by the direct vote of the citizens of the United States, without regard to whether the citizens are residents of a State." In common with similar proposals in earlier Congresses, this measure has been referred to the House Judiciary Committee's Subcommittee on the Constitution, but no further action has been scheduled. Given the prevalence of this pattern, it is arguable that there may be little congressional interest in devoting the high levels of time and energy demanded to consideration of an electoral college-related constitutional amendment in the foreseeable future.

Trends in Congressional Electoral College Reform Proposals

As noted previously, congressional interest in constitutional amendments to reform or eliminate the electoral college has declined in recent decades. From proposals offered in recent years, two trends emerge. First, nearly all relevant amendments would eliminate the electoral college and substitute direct popular election. No proposal to reform the electoral college has been introduced since the 107th Congress. Second, the scope of proposed direct popular election amendments is arguably evolving in complexity and detail.

It is unclear whether the first development reflects a decline in electoral college support, lack of interest in reform proposals, or simply the absence of a sense of urgency. It is possible that supporters of the current system in some form would coalesce to defend the electoral college, if its existence or integrity were endangered. Recent actions by the Heritage Foundation and the State Government Leadership Foundation, reported later in this report, arguably confirm this thesis.

Another trend is that recent proposals go beyond substituting direct election for the electoral college. Presidential election reform amendments in recent Congresses have frequently included provisions to enhance and extend federal authority in such areas as residence standards, definition of citizenship, national voter registration, inclusion of U.S. dependencies in the presidential election process, establishment of an election day holiday, ballot access standards for parties and candidates, etc. If approved and ratified, they would afford Congress authority to establish broad

---

[131] Congress responded with the Help America Vote Act, enacted in 2002. For additional information, please consult CRS Report RS20898, *The Help America Vote Act and Elections Reform: Overview and Issues,* by Kevin J. Coleman and Eric A. Fischer.

[132] U.S. Federal Election Commission, *2008 Official Presidential General Election Results,* available at http://www.fec.gov/pubrec/fe2008/2008presgeresults.pdf. One of the asserted advantages of the electoral college system is that the predominance of the general ticket system in the states tends to magnify the winning candidates' electoral vote margin. According to its defenders, this characteristic confers added legitimacy on the winning ticket and deters legal challenges to the popular vote results.

national election standards which would supersede current state and political party practices and requirements.

Congressional authority over federal elections stems from Article I Section 4, clause 1 of the Constitution for Congress, and Article II, Section 1, clause 4 for presidential electors. For further information and a detailed analysis of this authority, consult CRS Report RL30747, *Congressional Authority to Standardize National Election Procedures*, by Kenneth R. Thomas.

The prospect of increased federal involvement in the administration of presidential elections raises two potential issues. The first is whether such federal involvement in traditionally state and local practices might be considered an unfunded mandate, as it could impose additional costs on sub-federal governments. Indeed, bills that had the effect of imposing uncompensated costs on state and local election authorities might be subject to points of order on the floor of both the House and Senate.[133] One response by the affected governments might be to call for federal funding to meet the increased expenses imposed by federal requirements. Precedent for this exists in the grant program incorporated in the Help American Vote Act (HAVA).[134] A second issue centers on perceptions that such an amendment might be regarded as federal intrusion in state and local responsibilities. For instance, a far-reaching scenario might include the gradual assumption of the election administration structure by the federal government. In this hypothetical case, questions could be raised as to (1) the costs involved; (2) whether a national election administration system could efficiently manage all the varying nuances of state and local conditions; and (3) what would be the long-term implications for federalism? Conversely, it could be asserted that (1) a national or federal election administration structure is appropriate for national elections; (2) state or local concerns are counterbalanced by the urgent requirement that every citizen be enabled and encouraged to vote; and (3) every vote should be accurately counted.

Current Developments in Reform Initiatives—Activity in the States

Given the unlikely prospect of congressional action on electoral college reform, a variety of alternative plans has emerged over the past decade. While only a constitutional amendment can alter the fundamental arrangements of the electoral college, some elements of the system could be changed by the states. In this instance, the states would act, or have acted in the case of Maine and Nebraska in their adoption of the district plan, in their classic role as "laboratories of democracy." The Constitution, in Article II, Section 1, clause 2 requires that "Each State shall appoint, in such Manner as the Legislature thereof may direct, a Number of Electors, equal to the whole Number of Senators and Representatives to which the State may be entitled in Congress...."[135] In other words, the states are free to experiment with systems of elector selection and electoral vote allocation, up to a point. Over the past decade both proportional and congressional district plan proposals have been advanced in the states. A technical caveat to the reader: it should be recalled that, notwithstanding widespread usage, including in this report,

---

[133] For additional information, please consult CRS Report R40957, *Unfunded Mandates Reform Act: History, Impact, and Issues*, by Robert Jay Dilger and Richard S. Beth.

[134] Help America Vote Act (HAVA): P.L. 107-252; 116 Stat. 1666.

[135] This power is not, however, absolute. Federal court decisions have struck down state laws concerning appointment of electors that were found to be in violation of the 14th Amendment's guarantee of equal protection. For additional discussion, see *United States Constitution: Analysis and Interpretation Constitution Annotated)*, Article II, Section 1, Clauses 2-4. Available at http://www.crs.gov/products/conan/Article02/topic_S1_C2_1_2.html.

electoral votes are not awarded to particular candidates; rather, *electors pledged to support particular candidates are elected.*

Proportional Plan—Colorado Amendment 36, 2004

On November 2, 2004, Colorado voters rejected a state constitutional amendment that would have provided for proportional allocation of electoral votes.[136] Had the amendment passed and survived legal challenges, it would have provided proportional allocation of Colorado's presidential electors for 2004 and future presidential elections. After a spirited campaign that stirred some national interest, Amendment 36 was ultimately defeated by a vote of 697,000 in favor to 1,307,000 opposed.[137] For the record, if the amendment had been in effect for the 2008 election, the Democratic candidates Barack Obama and Joe Biden would have received five electoral votes, while the Republicans John McCain and Sarah Palin would have received four. Under the winner-take-all system, the Democratic ticket received all nine Colorado electoral votes.[138]

District Plan—California, 2008

Supporters of the district plan assert that it is an fairer alternative to the general ticket/winner-take-all system because in tallying popular votes by congressional district, it more accurately reflects voter preferences in different parts of a state, and by also counting them statewide, it recognizes the overall winners on the state level by awarding them the two "senatorial" electors. Results of the 2008 presidential election in Nebraska provide a real-world example of the district plan in action.[139] Republican candidates McCain and Palin won a majority of votes both in Nebraska's 1st and 3rd congressional districts, and statewide, while Democrats Obama and Biden won a majority in the 2nd congressional district. Under Nebraska's district plan, the Republican ticket took four electoral votes, one for each district, and two for the statewide total, while the Democrats took a single electoral vote, representing the 2nd congressional district.[140]

Earlier in the decade, district plan advocates in the Golden State proposed the California Presidential Reform Act (California Counts), a version similar to those used in Maine and Nebraska. They sought to have their proposal submitted to the voters under California's provision for enactment of legislation by popular initiative. Supporters noted that in 2004, Democratic nominees John Kerry and John Edwards received 54.3% of the popular vote, and all 55 electoral votes, while Republicans George Bush and Dick Cheney received 44.4% of the popular vote, but no electoral votes.[141] If the district system had been in place in California in 2004, Kerry-Edwards would have received 33 electoral votes (31 congressional districts, and 2 statewide electors, and

---

[136] Amendment 36, available at http://www.lawanddemocracy.org/pdffiles/COamend36.pdf.

[137] Colorado, Secretary of State, *Official Publication of the Abstract of Votes Cast for the 2003 Coordinated[,] 2005 Primary[,] 2004 General [Elections]* (n.p., n.d.), pp. 138-139.

[138] U.S. Congress, House, Clerk of the House of Representatives, *Statistics of the Presidential and Congressional Elections, November 4, 2008*, available at http://clerk.house.gov/member_info/electionInfo/2008/2008Stat.htm#stateCO.

[139] As noted earlier in this report, Maine and Nebraska both use a district system to award electoral votes.

[140] Nebraska, Secretary of State, *Official Results of Nebraska General Election, November 4, 2008*, p. 10; available at http://www.sos.ne.gov/elec/pdf/2008%20General%20Canvass%20Book.pdf, p. 10.

[141] *America at the Polls 26*, p. 28.

Bush-Cheney, 22 (22 congressional districts).[142] California Counts was the subject of heated political debate between Democrats and Republicans, and was also criticized on state constitutional grounds.[143] A greater obstacle was the need to gather supportive petitions from voters equal in number to 5% of votes cast in the most recent gubernatorial election, a total of 433,971 valid signatures of registered voters at that time.[144] The California Counts organization ultimately failed to obtain the necessary signatures, and the proposed act never appeared on the ballot in 2008.[145]

District Plan Proposals in Nebraska, Pennsylvania, and Wisconsin, 2011-2012

The district plan generated a renewed level of interest in a number of states in 2011 and 2012. Legislators in Nebraska introduced legislation to return that state to winner-take-all disposition of electoral votes, while a bill to move Pennsylvania into the district system was introduced in that state, and another was discussed in Wisconsin. None of these proposals received more than cursory action in their respective states, however.

Nebraska

On January 6, 2011, LB21, a bill to return Nebraska to the general ticket or winner-take-all system, was introduced in the unicameral legislature. Proponents asserted that the district plan had weakened the state's influence in national politics, while opponents claimed that it actually promoted grassroots involvement in elections and public affairs, and that the split electoral vote in 2008 proved the validity of the district plan.[146] Some commentators, however, suggested that the proposed change reflected Republican concerns that the district system had energized Democratic voters in the 2008 election, leading to closer results than anticipated in the statewide presidential vote and other election contests that year.[147] Although the bill was the subject of committee discussion, it was indefinitely postponed on April 18, 2012.[148]

---

[142] *Electoral College Vote by Congressional District, 1996-2004*, CRS Congressional Distribution Memorandum by Kevin J. Coleman, Royce Crocker, Dana Ely and Terrence Lisbeth, September 10, 2007, p. 3. For the record, in 2008 the district plan would have awarded 44 electoral votes (42 districts and 2 statewide electoral votes) to Obama and Biden, and 11 (11 congressional districts) to McCain and Palin. See "Election 08 Results by District," *CQ Politics*, available at http://innovation.cq.com/atlas/district_08.

[143] Vikram David Amar, "The So-Called Presidential Reform Act: A Clear Abuse of California's Initiative Process," *FindLaw Legal News and Commentary*, August 17, 2007, available at http://writ.news.findlaw.com/amar/20070817.html.

[144] Computed from California, Secretary of State, Elections Division, *Statement of Vote, 2006 General Election*, p. x, available at http://www.sos.ca.gov/elections/sov/2006_general/complete_sov.pdf.

[145] See, for example: Shane Goldmacher, "Electoral College Measure Falls Short," *Sacramento Bee Capitol Alert*, February 5, 2008, available at http://blogs.sacbee.com/capitolalertlatest/2008/02/electoral-colle.html.

[146] "Electoral College Changes Proposed," *Unicameral Update, the Nebraska Legislature's Official News Source*, February 24, 2011, available at http://update.legislature.ne.gov/?p=3539.

[147] Don Walton, "Electoral Vote Change Stuck in Committee," *JournalStar.com*, Lincoln *Journal-Star*, March 10, 2011, available at http://journalstar.com/news/unicameral/article_6b78c3da-95fc-54c0-8f12-486e5e8a9fff.html.

[148] See http://update.legislature.ne.gov/?p=3539.

Pennsylvania

A district plan proposal introduced in the Pennsylvania legislature later in 2011 generated considerably greater publicity and political controversy. On September 30, Senator Dominic Pileggi, majority leader of the Pennsylvania Senate, introduced Senate Bill 1282, which proposed to substitute the district plan for the general ticket system used in the Keystone State since the first presidential elections. The bill proposed a standard district system, with one elector apportioned to each congressional district, and two at-large, representing the "senatorial" electors. On election day, voters would cast a single vote for the electors pledged to their candidates, and these popular election results would be counted statewide. The ticket of candidates winning the most votes in the state would be awarded the two at-large electors, while the ticket winning in each congressional district would be awarded the single elector representing that district.[149] Senator Pileggi asserted that "[t]his proposal will more fairly align Pennsylvania's electoral college votes with the results of the popular vote. It will also make individual votes across the state more important, giving voters a more significant say in presidential elections."[150] Some observers, however, suggested the proposal was designed to break a 20-year Democratic hold on Pennsylvania's electoral college delegation.[151] In awarding electoral votes by congressional district, it was argued, Republicans might gain as many as 12 or 13 electoral votes from Republican-leaning districts under the district plan.[152] Opponents claimed the proposal was "a blatant power grab meant to rig presidential elections and diminish the voice of voters in Democratic strongholds."[153] Some Republicans also criticized the bill, on the grounds that the state Democratic Party organization might "move campaigns out of safe Democratic districts in urban population centers and into the more moderate suburbs."[154]

SB 1282 was referred to the Committee on State Government on September 30,[155] but by the end of November, interest in the proposal had waned; supporters indicated that SB 1282 was on hold, perhaps indefinitely.[156] No further action was taken during the 2012 legislative session.

---

[149] Senate Bill No. 1282, Amending the Act of June 3, 1937, Session of 2011, Pennsylvania General Assembly, available at http://www.legis.state.pa.us/cfdocs/billinfo/billinfo.cfm?syear=2011&sind=0&body=S&type=B&BN=1282.

[150] "Senator Pileggi Unveils Proposal to More Fairly Allocate Electoral College Votes," statement, September 13, 2011, available at http://www.senatorpileggi.com/press/2011/0911/091311.htm.

[151] Pennsylvania voted for Democratic presidential candidates for every election since 1992.

[152] Aaron Blake, "Could Pennsylvania Republicans End the Electoral College as We Know It?" *Washington Post*, September 14, 2011, available at http://www.washingtonpost.com/blogs/the-fix/post/could-pennsylvania-republicans-end-the-electoral-college-as-we-know-it/2011/09/14/gIQAQUzUSK_blog.html .

[153] Dan Hirschhorn, "House GOP Fret Over Pa. Electorals [sic]," *Politico*, September 14, 2011, available at http://www.politico.com/news/stories/0911/63522.html. Here again, Professor Lawrence Longley's "voting power" theory comes into play. Substantial concentrations of Democratic voters, particularly minority voters, in the Philadelphia and Pittsburgh metropolitan areas have long been regarded as a key element in gaining a Democratic plurality or majority in the popular vote in Pennsylvania. A district plan system for awarding electoral votes would arguably lessen the voting power of minority votes in the state by awarding as many as 12 to 13 electoral votes to congressional district electors from Republican-leaning districts in the state.

[154] "Pete Sessions: Pa. Electoral College Change Would Put House Races at Risk," *Wall Street Journal, Washington Wire*, September 15, 2011, available at http://blogs.wsj.com/washwire/2011/09/15/pete-sessions-pa-electoral-college-change-would-put-house-races-at-risk/.

[155] SB 1282, Regular Session, 2011-2012, Pennsylvania General Assembly, available at http://www.legis.state.pa.us/cfdocs/billinfo/billinfo.cfm?syear=2011&sind=0&body=S&type=B&BN=1282 .

[156] "Pennsylvania Electoral College Bill On Hold," *CBS Philly*, November 27, 2011, available at http://philadelphia.cbslocal.com/2011/11/27/pennsylvania-electoral-college-bill-on-hold/.

Wisconsin

Shortly after Pennsylvania's SB 182 was introduced, the *Milwaukee Journal Sentinel* reported that Wisconsin State Representative Daniel Le Mahieu was proposing district plan legislation for that state. Arguments in favor of and opposition to the proposal were similar to those raised in Pennsylvania.[157] Opponents, however, also claimed that the district plan would eliminate Wisconsin from the roster of "battleground" states. This, they asserted, would lead presidential campaign organizations and political parties to shift their resources to states where the winner-take-all system promised bigger electoral vote rewards for their campaign spending. Under this scenario, the district system would ultimately cost the state economy millions of dollars in broadcast TV revenue, and even more from lost radio, cable, travel, staff, and other campaign-related spending.[158] At the time of this writing, however, no such bill had been introduced in the legislature.[159]

The National Popular Vote Campaign: Direct Popular Election Through an Interstate Compact

The National Popular Vote (NPV) campaign movement seeks to establish direct popular election of the President and Vice President through an interstate compact, rather than by constitutional amendment. Under the compact's provisions, legislatures of the 50 states and the District of Columbia would appoint presidential electors committed to the presidential/vice presidential ticket *that gained the most votes nationwide*. This would deliver a unanimous electoral college decision for the candidates winning a plurality of the popular vote.

Northwestern University law professor Robert W. Bennett and constitutional scholars Akhil and Vikram Amar are generally credited as originators of the NPV concept.[160] Their proposal provides the basis of the National Popular Vote Plan. NPV relies on the Constitution's broad grant of power to each state to "appoint, *in such Manner as the Legislature thereof may direct* [emphasis added], a Number of Electors, equal to the whole Number of Senators and Representatives to which the State may be entitled in the Congress."[161]

Specifically, the plan calls for an interstate agreement or compact in which the legislature in each of the participating states agrees to appoint electors pledged to the candidates who won the *nationwide popular vote*. State election authorities would count and certify the popular vote in each state, which would be aggregated and certified nationwide as the "nationwide popular vote." The participating state legislatures would then choose the slate of electors pledged to the

---

[157] Craig Gilbert, "Changing the Way the Electoral College Works in Wisconsin: A Recipe for Irrelevance?" *Milwaukee Journal Sentinel, Journal Interactive*, October 23, 2011. Available at http://www.jsonline.com/blogs/news/132415248.html .

[158] Ibid.

[159] Wisconsin Legislative Documents website, available at https://docs.legis.wisconsin.gov/2011/related/author_index/assembly/A_LeMahieu_Daniel?view=section .

[160] Robert W. Bennett, "Popular Election of the President Without a Constitutional Amendment," *The Green Bag, An Entertaining Journal of Law*, 4 Green Bag 2d 241, available from the Social Science Research Network by subscription, see http://papers.ssrn.com/sol3/papers.cfm?abstract_id=261057; Akhil Reed Amar and Vikram David Amar, "How to Achieve Direct National Election of the President Without Amending the Constitution," *Findlaw's Writ*, December 28, 2001, available at http://writ.news.findlaw.com/amar/20011228.html .

[161] U.S. Constitution, Article II, Section 1, clause 2.

"nationwide popular vote winner," *notwithstanding the results within their particular state.*[162] Barring unforeseen circumstances, the NPV would ultimately result in a unanimous electoral college vote of 538 electors for the winning candidates. As a safety measure, the process would come into effect only after states whose total electoral votes equal or exceed a majority of 270 approve the plan. If the national popular vote were tied, the states would be released from their commitment under the compact, and choose electors who represented the presidential ticket that gained the most votes in each particular state. One novel NPV provision would enable the presidential candidate who won the national popular vote to fill any vacancies in the electoral college with electors of his or her own choice.

States would retain the right to withdraw from the compact, but if a state chose to withdraw within six months of the end of a presidential term, the withdrawal would not be effective until after the succeeding President and Vice President had been elected.

National Popular Vote, Inc.

The NPV advocacy effort is managed by National Popular Vote, Inc., a "501(c)(4)"[163] non profit corporation, established in California in 2006 by Barry Fadem, an attorney specializing in initiative and referendum law, and Stanford University professor John R. Koza.[164] As a 501(c)(4) entity, it is permitted to engage in political activity in furtherance of its goal, so long as this is not its primary activity. NPV's board members include former Senators and Representatives of both major political parties, suggesting bipartisan support on the national level. As of October 17, 2012, NPV claimed the support of 2,110 state legislators, over one sixth of the 7,382 total, and endorsements by the *New York Times*, *Los Angeles Times*, *Chicago Sun-Times*, *Minneapolis Star Tribune*, *Boston Globe*, *Miami Herald* and other newspapers.[165]

NPV Momentum?

According to NPV, the compact has been introduced in the legislatures of all 50 states, and the Council of the District of Columbia. By late 2011, eight states and the District of Columbia, possessing a total of 132 electoral votes, had adopted it. In chronological order with year of adoption, they are:

- **Hawaii** (4 electoral votes), 2008;

- **Illinois** (20 electoral votes), 2008;

- **Maryland** (10 electoral votes), 2008;

- **New Jersey** (14 electoral votes), 2008;

---

[162] Under NPV, assume that presidential ticket "A" won 55% of the popular vote in State "X," and ticket "B" won 45%. Under the current general ticket system, the state legislature would typically choose electors pledged to ticket A. Under NPV, assume the same in-state results, but assume that ticket "B" won the national popular vote. The state legislature, in compliance with the National Popular Vote compact, would vote to chose electors committed to ticket "B," because that ticket won the national popular vote, notwithstanding the in-state returns.

[163] 26 U.S.C. 501 (c)(4). Organizations recognized by the Internal Revenue Service under this provision of the IRS Code may lobby for legislation and participate in political campaigns and elections.

[164] Rick Lyman, "Innovator Devises Way Around Electoral College," *New York Times*, September 22, 2006, http://www.nytimes.com/2006/09/22/us/politics/22electoral.html.

[165] National Popular Vote website, available at http://www.nationalpopularvote.com/.

- **Washington** (12 electoral votes), 2009;

- **Massachusetts** (11 electoral votes), 2010;

- **District of Columbia** (3 electoral votes), 2010;

- **Vermont** (3 electoral votes), 2011; and

- **California** (55 electoral votes), 2011.

California's accession to the compact, finalized by Governor Edmund G. "Jerry" Brown on August 11, 2011, added 55 electoral votes to the total in states that have approved NPV, and brought it to 49% of its 270-vote operational threshold. The compact was under active consideration in the legislatures of 11 additional states which collectively cast an additional 124 electoral votes, but there were no further state approvals during the 2011-2012 state legislative sessions.

In another development, on February 23, 2011, businessman, philanthropist, and former three-time New York gubernatorial candidate Tom Golisano, announced that he would become a spokesman for the National Popular Vote campaign, and, according to press accounts, would "bankroll" NPV efforts.[166] Perhaps in response to perceived NPV momentum, defenders of the existing arrangements have begun measures to protect the electoral college system. On December 7, 2011, the Heritage Foundation, a conservative public policy institute, hosted a forum at which guest speakers, including five state secretaries of state, expressed their concern over the National Popular Vote campaign.[167] On December 8, *Roll Call* reported that the State Government Leadership Foundation, a project of the Republican State Leadership Committee, would begin a campaign to defend the electoral college and counter recent NPV gains.[168]

National Popular Vote: Pro and Con

Arguments in support of and opposed to the National Popular Vote proposal resemble those for and against direct popular election; the central issue turns on the question of the simplicity, logic, and democratic attractiveness of the direct election idea as compared to a more complex array of factors cited by supporters of the electoral college system.

Arguments Favoring the NPV Compact

The National Popular Vote movement advocates the NPV compact on the grounds of fairness and respect for the voters' choice. According to NPV, the central argument in favor is that the compact "would guarantee the Presidency to the candidate who receives the most popular votes [or at least

---

[166] Joseph Spector, "Tom Golisano to Lead National Popular Vote Effort," *WGRZ.com* (Buffalo, New York), February 23, 2011, available at http://www.wgrz.com/news/article/110466/1/Tom-Golisano-to-Lead-National-Popular-Vote-Effort . Hendrik Hertzberg, "N.P.V. Gets a Boost," *The New Yorker* (Blogs), March 14, 2011, available at http://www.newyorker.com/online/blogs/hendrikhertzberg/2011/03/npv-gets-a-boost.html .

[167] Heritage Foundation, "The Electoral College and the National Popular Vote Plan," available at http://www.heritage.org/events/2011/12/electoral-college .

[168] Eliza Newlin Carney, "GOP Nonprofit Backs Electoral College," *Roll Call.com*, December 8, 2011, available at http://www.rollcall.com/issues/57_71/GOP-Nonprofit-Backs-Electoral-College-210872-1.html. For further information on the State Government Leadership Foundation and its election law-related activities, see the foundation's website at, http://www.sglf.org/election-law.

a plurality] in all 50 states (and the District of Columbia)."[169] It also eliminates (1) the possibility of Presidents who won fewer votes than their opponent; (2) faithless electors; (3) "disfranchisement" under the winner-take-all system; (4) the various "voting power" advantages noted earlier in this report; and (5) the potential for contingent election under the 12th Amendment.[170]

In addition to the argument to fairness and democratic principle, NPV also asserts it would provide a practical benefit to non-"battleground states," encouraging presidential nominees and their organizations to spread their presence and resources more evenly as they campaigned for every vote nationwide, rather than concentrate on winning key "battleground" states:

> candidates have no reason to poll, visit, organize, campaign, or worry about the concerns of voters of states that they cannot possibly win or lose. This means that voters in two thirds of the states are effectively disenfranchised in presidential elections because candidates concentrate their attention on a small handful of "battleground" states. In 2004, candidates concentrated over two-thirds of their money and campaign visits in just five states; over 80% in nine states, and over 99% of their money in just 16 states.[171]

For instance, they note that California voters seldom see the presidential or vice presidential nominees or benefit from campaign spending because the Golden State is considered to be reliably Democratic, so Democratic candidates are said to take its 55 electoral votes for granted, and Republican candidates make few appearances in support of an apparently hopeless cause. Similar arguments on the Republican side apply to Texas, a state that has voted for Republican presidential nominees since 1980. Opponents might argue that spreading campaign spending resources in non-battleground states is a questionable goal with which to justify such a profound change in the presidential election process. Campaign appearances and spending, they might assert, should not be considered to be a local economic stimulus package, nor are the amounts in question sufficient to make much of a difference in the economic condition of most states. Moreover, they might continue, it is equally dubious to assert that nominees will slight the concerns of citizens of the states from which they draw their greatest support, or that concentrated campaigning in the "battleground" states somehow "disenfranchises" voters in others. In the modern era, only a tiny percentage of voters ever actually see a presidential or vice presidential candidate from either party. Television, the Internet, and newspapers, not rallies and torchlight parades, and word of mouth, are the dominant sources of voters' information on the campaign today.

Arguments Opposing the NPV Compact

Opponents may assert that NPV would undermine the Constitution and overturn the Founders' original intent. As noted earlier in this report, they could argue that presidential elections are not only national, but federal, contests, in which the states have an important role. The electoral college is an integral and important component of federalism, against which national popular election would be a serious blow. From a practical standpoint, they might argue that NPV would

---

[169] National Popular Vote website, available at http://www.nationalpopularvote.com/pages/explanation.php.

[170] Contingent election takes place under the existing system if no candidates receive a majority of electoral votes. For further information, please consult CRS Report RL32695, *Election of the President and Vice President by Congress: Contingent Election*, by Thomas H. Neale.

[171] National Popular Vote website, available at http://www.nationalpopularvote/com/pages/explanation.php.

lead to an increase in contested election results and legal challenges in the states, as the political parties maneuver to claim every possible vote.

Another point in opposition could be that NPV is an admitted "end run" around the Constitution,[172] that seeks fundamental change in the nation's election structure by circumventing the amendment process established by the Founders in Article V of the Constitution. Proponents may argue that Article V presents too high a hurdle for what they consider a necessary reform of the system, but opponents would likely assert that the Founders intended to make it difficult to alter provisions of the nation's fundamental charter. NPV, they could assert, seeks to circumvent these safeguards, and in this sense, it is anti-constitutional, if not unconstitutional.

Critics may also note that the National Popular Vote plan contains no "statute of limitations," unlike constitutional amendments which must be approved by three-fourths of the states, typically within a seven-year period.[173] Where, critics may ask, is a similar time limit that would "sunset" the National Popular Vote compact, after which it NPV would expire, or return to "square one?" According to its website, NPV was launched on February 23, 2006;[174] if it were a constitutional amendment, it would expire after February 23, 2013, if not adopted by three-fourths of the states. By what reasoning, they might argue, should the NPV be exempt from the standards Congress sets for constitutional amendments?

Ultimately, opponents could argue, NPV uses anti-democratic means to secure a democratic goal. Once the NPV compact is operational, the will of the citizens of any state, as expressed in their vote, will be immaterial when compared with the nationwide popular vote total—legislatures would be compelled by the compact to appoint electors pledged to the nationwide winners, notwithstanding the preference expressed by the voters of their state. Barring unforeseen circumstances, the electoral vote under NPV would always be 538 for the ticket winning the most popular votes nationwide to 0 for the runners-up, no matter how many states they carried. Opponents might note that results like these would be more characteristic of a totalitarian "people's democracy" than a democratic federal republic like the United States, and might lead to the very sort of constitutional crisis NPV was intended to avoid.

National Popular Vote: Legal and Constitutional Issues

Some observers have questioned the constitutionality of the National Popular Vote plan. Derek T. Muller, writing in *Election Law Journal*, asserts that NPV is an interstate compact within the meaning of the Constitution, and that it must be approved by Congress before taking effect.[175] Certain types of interstate agreements or compacts, he notes, do not require the explicit consent of Congress "because they do not affect national sovereignty or concern the core meaning of the

---

[172] This is the term applied by NPV founder, John Koza, in a 2006 interview: "When people complain that it's an end run," Dr. Koza said, "I just tell them, 'Hey, an end run is a legal play in football.'" Rick Lyman, "Innovator Devises Way Around Electoral College." *New York Times*, September 22, 2006, available at http://www.nytimes.com/2006/09/22/us/politics/22electoral.html .

[173] Congress has set the seven-year period as a reasonable time limit for the ratification process for the 18th, 20th, and all succeeding amendments.

[174] See National Popular Vote website, available at http://www.nationalpopularvote.com/pages/summary.php .

[175] "No State shall, without the consent of Congress, ... enter into any Agreement or Compact with another State, or with a foreign Power.... " Article I, Section 10, clause 3.

Compact Clause."[176] He maintains, however, that the National Popular Vote agreement would require explicit congressional approval because it binds the states to a particular course of action, places time limits on their ability to withdraw from NPV, and meets or exceeds conditions historically found to define "interstate compacts" by the Supreme and other U.S. Courts.[177] Muller further maintains that the NPV concept is inherently unconstitutional unless specifically approved by Congress because it would enhance the political power of participating states, at the expense of those that did not join the compact:

> States have an interest in appointing their electors as they see fit, and the Presidential Electors Clause of the Constitution grants this exclusive authority to the states. Technically, the non-compacting sister states can still appoint electors, but the Interstate Compact makes such an appointment meaningless. The outcome of the Electoral College would be determined by an arranged collective agreement among compacting states, regardless of what non-compacting states do about it.... This evisceration of political effectiveness is a sufficient interest to invoke the constitutional safeguard of congressional consent.[178]

The National Popular Vote movement agrees that NPV is an interstate compact, but it maintains that the Constitution implicitly permits valid interstate agreements without the need for congressional approval on any subject that falls within the states' constitutional authority.[179] NPV further notes that since the compact concerns the states' undisputed discretion as to the method by which they appoint electors, it would therefore be an appropriate subject for an interstate compact.[180] Finally, they assert that the Supreme Court twice rejected arguments that an interstate compact was unconstitutional because "it impaired the sovereign rights of nonmember states or enhanced the political power of the member states at the expense of other states," as has been asserted by NPV opponents.[181]

Other critics claim the National Popular Vote compact might violate Sections 2 and 5 of the Voting Rights Act (VRA). Writing in *Columbia Law Review*, David Gringer invokes the voting power theory.[182] He argues that the plan conflicts with Section 2 of VRA because moving from "a state-based [vote] to a national popular vote dilutes the voting strength of a given state's minority population by reducing its ability [voting power] to influence the outcome of presidential elections."[183] Gringer also asserts that the NPV compact may violate Section 5 of the act, which restrains "covered"[184] jurisdictions from implementing changes to "any voting qualification or

---

[176] Derek T. Muller, "The Compact Clause and the National Popular Vote Interstate Compact," *Election Law Journal*, vol. 8, no. 4 (n.d.), 2007, p. 382. Examples include the multi-state "EZ-Pass" auto toll agreement, and the northeastern states Regional Greenhouse Gas Initiative.

[177] Ibid., pp. 388-389.

[178] Ibid., p. 391.

[179] John R. Koza, Barry Fadem, et al. *Every Vote Equal: A State-Based Plan for Electing the President by National Popular Vote* (Los Altos, CA: National Popular Vote Press, 2006), pp. 284-285.

[180] Koza, Fadem, et al., *Every Vote Equal*, pp. 284-285.

[181] Ibid., citing *U.S. Steel Corp. v. Multistate Tax Commission*, 434 U.S. 452, 494 n. 23 (1978) (White dissenting), and *Northeast Bancorp, Inc. v. Board of Governors of the Federal Reserve System*, 472 U.S. 159, 176 (1985).

[182] As noted earlier, the voting power theory holds that a state's influence depends on the size of its electoral college delegation, and its consequent ability to influence the outcome of an election. For a fuller explanation of voting power, see Lawrence D. Longley and Neal R. Peirce, *The Electoral College Primer 2000* (Yale University Press, New Haven: 1999), pp. 149-161.

[183] David Gringer, "Why the National Popular Vote Plan is the Wrong Way to Abolish the Electoral College, *Columbia Law Review*, vol. 108, 2008, p. 208.

[184] Covered jurisdictions were defined in the act as effectively those in which there was evidence of discrimination (continued...)

---

prerequisite to voting, or *standard, practice, or procedure* (emphasis added) with respect to voting,"[185] until the proposed change has been reviewed for potential discriminatory intent, a process known as preclearance. He argues that the NPV compact would qualify as a covered practice under Section 5, and that the legislatures of all the "covered" states would need to obtain preclearance before implementing the compact.[186]

Responding to this point, NPV noted that

> The National Popular Vote bill manifestly would make every person's vote for President equal throughout the United States in an election to fill a single office (the Presidency). It is entirely consistent with the goal of the Voting Rights Act. There have been court cases under the Voting Rights Act concerning contemplated changes in voting methods for various representative legislative bodies.... However, these cases do not bear on elections to fill a single office (i.e., the Presidency)."[187]

It should, however, be noted that in 2012, the Justice Department's Civil Rights Division specifically declined to challenge California's accession to the NPV on Voting Rights Act grounds.[188]

Finally, it may be noted that the states' authority to appoint electors by any method their legislatures choose is not absolute. Federal court decisions have struck down state laws concerning appointment of electors that were found to be in violation of the 14th Amendment's guarantee of equal protection:

> Although Clause 2 (of Article II, Section 1 of the Constitution) seemingly vests complete discretion in the states, certain older cases had recognized a federal interest in protecting the integrity of the process. Thus, the Court upheld the power of Congress to protect the right of all citizens who are entitled to vote to lend aid and support in any legal manner to the election of any legally qualified person as a presidential elector.... [I]n *Oregon v. Mitchell* (42 U.S. 112 (1970)), the Court upheld the power of Congress to reduce the voting age in presidential elections and to set a thirty-day durational residency period as a qualification for voting in presidential elections. Although the Justices were divided on the reasons, the rationale emerging from this case, considered with *Williams v. Rhodes*, (393 U.S. 20 1968)) is that the Fourteenth Amendment limits state discretion in prescribing the manner of selecting electors and that Congress in enforcing the Fourteenth Amendment may override state practices that violate that Amendment and may substitute standards of its own.[189]

It is beyond the scope of this report to speculate on the outcome of these asserted legal and constitutional issues concerning the National Popular Vote compact, but the fact that they have

---

(...continued)

against minority voting rights in the years prior to passage of the original Voting Rights Act in 1965. They include eight states and local jurisdictions in another eight, located largely, though not exclusively, in the south.

[185] 42 U.S.C. 1973c.

[186] Gringer, "Why the National Popular Vote Plan is the Wrong Way to Abolish the Electoral College," p.188.

[187] National Popular Vote, *Myths About the National Popular Vote*, "18.1 Myths About the Voting Rights Act," http://www.nationalpopularvote.com/pages/answers/m18.php.

[188] U.S. Department of Justice, Civil Rights Division, Letter of T. Christian Herren, Jr., Chief, Voting Rights Section, at, http://www.fairvote.org/assets/NewFolder/Chapter-188-approval-letter-from-DOJ.pdf.

[189] For additional discussion, see *United States Constitution: Analysis and Interpretation Constitution Annotated)*, Article II, Section 1, Clauses 2-4. Available at http://www.crs.gov/products/conan/Article02/topic_S1_C2_1_2.html.

---

been identified and noted suggests the possibility of court challenges to the compact in the event that NPV were to approach or meet its 270 electoral vote threshold.

The Electoral College Outlook for 2012 and Beyond

There is little likelihood of major changes to the electoral college system in the immediate future by any of the three processes cited in this report—constitutional amendment, state legislation changing electoral vote formulae, or through the interstate compact proposed by the National Popular Vote campaign.

- From the standpoint of a constitutional amendment, there was little indication of congressional interest in the question during the 112th Congress. Although a direct popular election amendment or amendments will likely be introduced in the 113th Congress, barring such unforeseen circumstances as an electoral college "misfire," or some other election contest following the 2012 presidential election, there is little likelihood of action beyond introduction and pro forma committee referral.

- The states may continue to consider legislative action providing for changes in their procedures for allocating electoral votes, especially the district system. Barring unforeseen circumstances, however, such experiments do not appear to enjoy widespread support, and even if enacted, might be subject to serious criticism, and could result in legal challenges on various grounds, including dilution of minority voter influence.

- Finally, the National Popular Vote campaign, despite its successes in 2011, may have lost momentum, as it has in the past. If the 2012 presidential election results are uneventful, further action seems unlikely. Here again, however, an electoral college "misfire" or some other election contest could provide fresh impetus to the NPV interstate compact campaign.

Conclusion

The issues discussed in this report are not the only ones affecting contemporary presidential elections. As the report and the sources cited herein suggest, presidential elections are the subject of substantial scholarly study, media and public interest, and governmental activity. The three major topics discussed here—the nominating process, campaign finance, and the electoral college—are, however, among the most enduring issues in presidential elections. All three remain highly relevant for 2012. In each case, major changes to presidential selection have occurred since 2008 or are under consideration. Many of the developments discussed above will require additional time to fully understand, perhaps even beyond completion of the 2012 election cycle (especially for proposed changes to the electoral college). Nonetheless, history suggests that each of these areas will continue to be pillars of the presidential election process.

With these potentially major developments in mind, this report provides Congress with background about how and why contemporary presidential elections occur as they do. The process for selecting presidents has remained more or less unchanged since the 19th century. Generally speaking, that trend is likely to continue. The topics discussed here could nonetheless set the boundaries for how today's citizens, candidates, political parties, and outside groups participate in presidential elections. Members of Congress can and do participate in the politics and elections surrounding presidential selection. Congress also has unique responsibilities for overseeing federal roles in that process, which requires an understanding of how presidential elections evolved. This report provides a resource for doing so.

Author Contact Information

Kevin J. Coleman
Analyst in Elections
kcoleman@crs.loc.gov, 7-7878

R. Sam Garrett
Specialist in American National Government
rgarrett@crs.loc.gov, 7-6443

Thomas H. Neale
Specialist American National Government
tneale@crs.loc.gov, 7-7883